NOW THAT I'VE CAST IT, WHAT DO I DO WITH IT?

MAXINE TAYLOR

Cover Design by envisionarydesigns.com
Interior Design by bigAdesigns.com
Photo by Rob Melvin

TABLE OF CONTENTS

CONTENTS   PAGE

INTRODUCTION

BACK IN 1966, WHEN I BEGAN studying astrology, we had to cast (calculate) our charts by hand because computers were not yet available for this purpose. For the astrology student, this was a time-consuming process, and it was easy to make mistakes in the calculation of the birth chart. Because casting the chart was the first step, and because it was tedious, those of my students who mastered it felt a great sense of accomplishment. However, their immediate question was, "Now that I've cast it what do I *do* with it?" I wrote this book in answer to that question.

Back in the '60s, there were very few astrology books available for the serious student, and those that *were* available were not only hard to understand, but were negative in their interpretation of the birth chart. I spent a great deal of money on these books, but was often frustrated by their archaic language and negativity.

After teaching astrology for a few years, I realized that my students possessed the best book in the world: their own mind. All I had to do was simplify chart interpretation and make it practical and logical, and my students would be able to read any chart at all. This was the other reason I wrote this book.

If you are reading this book, you are looking for a logical, easy-to-understand way to read a chart. You are ready to take the difficulty and mystery out of chart interpretation. You are ready to use your own mind rather than someone else's ideas. You are ready to soar!

Now That I've Cast It, **What** *Do I Do With It?* is designed to give you the confidence you need to awaken the astrologer within you. Grab it and run with it!

Maxine

THE SYMBOLS

Aries (Ruler: ♂) *Mars*   ☉ Sun

Taurus (Ruler: ♀) *Venus*   ☽ Moon

Gemini (Ruler: ☿) *Mercury*   ☿ Mercury

Cancer (Ruler: ☽) *Moon*   ♀ Venus

Leo (Ruler: ☉) *Sun*   ♂ Mars

Virgo (Ruler: ☿) *Mercury*   ♃ Jupiter

Libra (Ruler: ♀) *Venus*   ♄ Saturn

Scorpio (Rulers: ♇ ♂) *pluto | Mars*   ♅ Uranus

Sagittarius (Ruler: ♃) *Jupiter*   ♆ Neptune

Capricorn (Ruler: ♄) *Saturn*   ♇ Pluto

Aquarius (Rulers: ♅ ♄) *uranus / Saturn*

Pisces (Rulers: ♆ ♃) *Neptune / Jupiter*   ☊ North Node

    ☋ South Node

    ☌ Conjunction

    ☍ Opposition

    □ Square

    ⅄ Quincunx

    Δ Trine

    ✶ Sextile

Handwritten annotations in left margin:

3/21 –

3/21 – 4/19 (Aries)

4/20 – 5/20 (Taurus)

5/21 – 6/21 (Gemini)

6/21 – 7/22 (Cancer)

7/23 – 8/22 (Leo)

8/23 – 9/22 (Virgo)

9/23 – 10/22 (Libra)

10/23 – 11/21 (Scorpio)

11/22 – 12/21 (Sagittarius)

12/22 – 1/19 (Capricorn)

1/20 – 2/18 (Aquarius)

2/19 – 3/20 (Pisces)

THE HOUSES

WHEN INTERPRETING A CHART, the things to look at, in order of importance are:
1) Planets in Houses (and Signs on Cusps)
2) Planets in Signs
3) Aspects Between Planets

Before we can interpret the planets in the houses, we must understand the meaning of the houses themselves. The best way to understand a particular house is to think of the sign which rules it in the natural zodiac because that sign will color the house with its own personality. For example, suppose someone has three planets in Aquarius in the 7th house. In spite of the fact that those planets are in Aquarius, there will be a strong Libran tone to the chart because of Libra's natural rulership of the 7th house. Another important point is that a planet falling in its "own" house will be much stronger than in another. This holds true no matter what sign it is in. For example, let's suppose that someone has Venus in Capricorn in the 2nd house. Venus is in its "own" house because of Taurus' natural rulership over the 2nd house (Venus rules Taurus).

♈
1st House

The 1st house rules the personality, physical appearance, physical body and personal mannerisms. The person with 1st house planets is a disguised Aries— the "me first" quality predominates. He is not intentionally selfish. It is just that, as far as he is concerned, he comes first. Period. Because his personality is strongly developed and his appearance can be quite striking, others will be attracted to him. While he enjoys the attention, he does not want to feel obligated or restricted. He needs to be free to throw himself into a new project at a moment's notice. If anyone blocks his path, he will take on the challenger by intensifying his efforts and ramming through the obstacle.

(Note: The 1st house is what you send out; the 7th is the way others see you in the one-on-one situation.)

♉
2nd House

The 2nd house describes the basic need in all of us for fulfillment of our personal desires. It also describes the tangible possessions (people or things) which we often substitute when our personal desires go unfulfilled. Because of Taurus' rulership over this house, the 2nd house person's needs are often very practical, and deal with the basic needs of life: food, shelter, love and the money to buy what he needs. Many people, however, have fulfilled their basic needs sufficiently enough so that they are working on fulfilling their secondary needs. For this reason, the 2nd house deals with our values, our priorities and all security-giving possessions.

♊
3rd House

This Gemini-influenced house deals with the concrete mind, ideas, memory and communication, including the manner in which we actually think and speak. It rules our childhood and the people who played a part in it, especially our siblings. A person with planets in the 3rd house is never at a loss for words (or ideas), and can talk as much as any Gemini. Since this house is the house of communication, the 3rd house person may not necessarily come up with the idea, but can hear it and then communicate it. This gives the 3rd house person the ability to mimic. The 3rd house rules short trips, and the person with a strong 3rd house loves to get in his car at least once a day, if only to drive around the block. He just has to keep moving or he can get bored, nervous and jumpy.

♋

4th House

Because of its relationship to Cancer, the 4th house triggers our deep emotional need for personal security. While most astrology students know that the 4th house is related to the home, family and real estate, they are not always aware of the emotional importance of this house. The cusp of the 4th is the foundation on which the entire chart is built, and determines the strength of the whole structure. If our security needs are fulfilled, our structure is sound. If we go through life unfulfilled on this deepest of all levels, our structure can suffer because we will be constantly trying to firm up our foundation to compensate for any lack therein. Who fulfills this security need? That is where the home and family come in, but most importantly, the parent described by the 4th house and the planets found there. Often, in the past, this was the mother because she, traditionally, spent more time at home. However, today, this does not always apply. More and more, mother is getting out of the home (4th house) to pursue a career (10th house). This raises the question: is mother the 4th and father the 10th, or vice-versa? That depends on the chart, and will vary from person to person. The importance of the 4th and 10th houses cannot be overstated, for these houses relate to our parents, and their influence in our lives is enormous. Since the 4th house also rules the second half of life, it may be that our security needs are fulfilled at that time by someone other than the 4th house parent.

There is a strong relationship between the 4th and 10th houses because our need for power and authority (10th house) can be strongly influenced by our need for emotional security (4th house). If our 4th house needs are unfulfilled, we may compensate for them in our 10th house.

♌
5ᵗʰ House

Because it is ruled by Leo in the natural zodiac, the 5ᵗʰ house deals with our creative urges and how we express them. It is the outward expression of the 2ⁿᵈ house of desire, and shows how we have fun—mentally, emotionally and physically. For this reason, and because the 5ᵗʰ house deals with all sorts of amusements, hobbies and sexual and social activities, I refer to it as the house of "fun and games". The person with planets in the 5ᵗʰ loves all sorts of amusements, from sports to cocktail parties. He also likes any kind of speculation, from gambling to investing.

The 5ᵗʰ house deals with children and all things we create. People with a strong 5ᵗʰ house attract children because they know how to play. Often, our pets are our children. Even a parent can be our child. The 5ᵗʰ house deals with schools which, ideally, encourage us to develop our creative abilities.

The 5ᵗʰ house rules drama and the theater, and the person with 5ᵗʰ house planets is dramatic—even in everyday situations. He has a flair for the elegant that makes even humdrum events come alive.

♍
6ᵗʰ House

This house deals with work, health and service, but like Virgo, the natural ruler of the 6ᵗʰ, the person with planets here does not just want to keep busy. He wants to provide some necessary service. He is only happy when he is useful, busy and needed. Because of this, he doesn't mind taking care of the small details of a project. He knows how important those details are to its success— and he realizes that no one else is willing to handle them. Perhaps this is why the 6ᵗʰ house rules small matters and loose ends.

The 6ᵗʰ house illustrates the relationship between our health and our job. (The 10ᵗʰ is the career; the 6ᵗʰ rules the job or actual service performed.) When things go wrong at work, our health can suffer. Perhaps we are having difficulty with an employee or co-worker. The 6ᵗʰ house rules these people. Our diet plays a major role in determining our health, and the 6ᵗʰ house rules this area as well.

The 6ᵗʰ house rules small animals. (Large animals are ruled by the 12ᵗʰ.) However, some people regard their pets as children, in which case, they should be read in the 5ᵗʰ house.

♎︎
7ᵗʰ House

The 7ᵗʰ house deals with interpersonal relationships of all kinds. The person with planets in the 7ᵗʰ lives for and through his partner, and prefers to deal one-to-one in all interactions. Like Libra, the 7ᵗʰ house person is looking for his "other half" in order to complete his life. The 7ᵗʰ house also deals with litigation, the lower courts, contracts, treaties, deals, contests, rivalry, competition, open enemies, the public, war, and harmony or separation. For example, after finding our mate (7ᵗʰ), and signing a marriage contract (7ᵗʰ), the harmony between us (7ᵗʰ) often changes and we begin to compete (7ᵗʰ) with each other. Our spouse (7ᵗʰ) then becomes our open enemy (7ᵗʰ), so we return to the courts (7ᵗʰ) in order to separate (7ᵗʰ) and divorce (7ᵗʰ). Remember that business partnerships are ruled by this house as well as those momentary one-on-one situations we encounter in our daily activities. The 7th house reflects the lesson of Libra—we either share or we separate.

♏︎
8th House

The 8th house is one of the most powerful houses in the zodiac because it is the house of transformation and resurrection. Whatever planets are in the 8th house will undergo a total regeneration and, like the Phoenix rising on its own ashes, will be born again on their highest level. Scorpio, the natural ruler of the 8th, is a sign of extremes, and to an 8th house person, life is "all or nothing".

The 8th house rules the secrets of life. As a result, 8th house people are often entrusted with others' secrets. This house deals with control, and the 8th house person often learns to manipulate in order to maintain control. Once he sees that he is controlled by the need to control, he is able to let it go and take charge of his life.

The 8th house rules deep desire, psychic energy and the astral plane. Mundanely, it rules debts, loans, joint finances, legacies and inheritances.

♐︎
9th House

Just like Sagittarius, its natural ruler, the 9th house deals with truth, honesty, our principles, beliefs and philosophy of life. It rules higher education, shows us our higher mind and reveals our attitude toward God. (Not religion; God.) The person with a strong 9th house wants to expand his horizons on all levels. This can be accomplished through higher education (9th house) or long distance travel (9th house)—either in or out of the body. (The 8th rules dreams; the 9th rules the trip we take during sleep.) This house rules publishing, foreign lands and foreigners. (It is interesting to note here that traditional astrology gives the 9th house rulership over in-laws as well!) It also rules foreign trade, justice, the law and the higher courts. Think of Sagittarius, and you'll understand the 9th house's need to expand.

I have found a correlation between the 9th house and the career, which is traditionally a 10th house matter. We study for our career in our 9th house of higher education, and the 10th is what the public sees of it (our public image).

♑

10th House

Just like Capricorn, the 10th house person wants to be on top and have a good public image. The 10th house rules the leader, the authority figure, and the 10th house person wants to BE the authority figure. He has an equally strong need to be respected and admired. Conversely, he finds it difficult to accept direction from anyone in authority who he does not respect.

The 10th house rules what the public sees of our career. It rules our reputation, the honors we win, our standing in the community, our public image. People with a strong 10th house naturally gravitate to positions of authority. This house also describes anyone who might be considered an authority figure, for example, a parent or boss.

The 10th house in a mundane chart rules the government and politics. It deals with the test in the use of power. If you have planets in the 10th, you may be placed in a position of authority in order to learn how to deal with power.

The 10th house rules the out-front parent, the one who receives attention and teaches the child how to behave in public.

♒
11th House

According to traditional astrology, this house deals with friends, groups, hopes and wishes. You might expect, then, that the 11th house person would have many friends. However, such is not always the case. Aquarius, the humanitarian, rules the natural 11th house, and there are two types of Aquarian: one type likes people, but doesn't need them. Rather than having many friends, he prefers to BE a friend whenever needed. The other type loves group activities and is always joining clubs, organizations and any gathering of more than two people. These two types of Aquarian are reflected in the two types of 11th house people. Both types, however, believe in the welfare of the group and feel that whatever is best for the group is ultimately best for them. This is often the reverse of how the other signs think.

The 11th house also deals with legislative bodies and other people's children, including adopted children and step-children.

♓

12ᵗʰ House

The 12ᵗʰ house seems to function on two levels. Those with planets in the 12ᵗʰ are either very spiritual, sacrificing people, or "escape artists" who retreat to the privacy of their own world in order to avoid the heaviness of reality and responsibility. The 12ᵗʰ house person, like the Piscean, wants to identify with something greater than himself. He wants to find a oneness with God. The spiritual type serves God by serving mankind. The other type can simply be a martyr who bemoans his fate and indulges in self-pity. While all 12ᵗʰ house people need to be alone at least once a day, the martyr carries this to an extreme by daydreaming, sleeping and indulging himself on all levels. The 12ᵗʰ house rules behind-the-scenes activities and places, such as hospitals, institutions, etc. The spiritual type works in these places, while the escapist type can retreat to them. The 12ᵗʰ house rules our hidden strengths and weaknesses, our subconscious mind, and our self-doing or –undoing. In addition, it rules large animals and hidden enemies, real or imagined.

SIGNS ON THE CUSPS

PLANETS ARE THE ROVING DELEGATES or representatives of the signs. Each sign represents a principle to
be learned. The house cusp on which a sign falls indi-
cates the area of life in which we will learn that principle. Al-
though we know the meanings of the signs, it is sometimes difficult to apply these meanings to the different areas of life. The
BASIC SENTENCE can simplify this process. If you think
of the qualities of each of the signs and compose a few BA-
SIC SENTENCES to describe them, it is easy to apply them
around the chart. The sentences I offer are merely suggestions.
Feel free to compose your own. *(Note: On occasion, a sentence
may need a slight modification in order to fit a particular cusp.)*

♈

Aries on the Cusps

Aries is the principle of Beginnings. Wherever Aries falls in your chart is where you want to do your thing NOW. It is that area of life in which you throw yourself into activity. Aries wants to be first, so the area of life in which it falls comes first to us.

Basic Sentences

_____ *comes first.*
You are impatient about _____.
You throw yourself into _____.

Aries on the 1ˢᵗ Cusp—(Since this is the house that Aries rules in the natural zodiac, its qualities are intensified here.) You come first. You are impatient. You throw yourself into whatever you want.

Aries on the 2ⁿᵈ Cusp—Your own values come first. You are impatient about money matters. You throw yourself into earning/spending money.

Aries on the 3ʳᵈ Cusp—Speaking your mind comes first. You are impatient to express your ideas. You throw yourself into your ideas.

Aries on the 4ᵗʰ Cusp—Security comes first. You are impatient to find security. You throw yourself into home and family projects.

Aries on the 5ᵗʰ Cusp—Your children come first. You are impatient with children. You throw yourself into fun activities.

Aries on the 6th Cusp—Your work comes first. You are impatient with employees. You throw yourself into your work.

Aries on the 7th Cusp—Partnership comes first. You are impatient with others. You throw yourself into partnerships.

Aries on the 8th Cusp—Being in control comes first. Your impatience and anger will be transformed in this lifetime. You throw yourself into situations of control.

Aries on the 9th Cusp—Your principles come first. You are impatient to travel. You throw yourself into your beliefs and principles.

Aries on the 10th Cusp—Your career comes first. You are impatient to be on top. You throw yourself into positions of authority.

Aries on the 11th Cusp—Your friends comes first. You are impatient to fulfill your hopes and wishes. You throw yourself into group activities.

Aries on the 12th Cusp—Your privacy comes first. There is a hidden impatience about you. You throw yourself into behind-the-scenes activities.

♉
Taurus on the Cusps

Practical Taurus teaches us our values and makes us tenacious of our possessions. Wherever Taurus falls in your chart is where you hang on for security. It also shows that area of life about which you feel very deeply.

Basic Sentences

You hang onto _____ for security.
You are practical about _____.
You feel very deeply about _____.

Taurus on the 1ˢᵗ Cusp—You hang onto yourself. You are practical. You feel things very deeply.

Taurus on the 2ⁿᵈ Cusp—(Since this is the house that Taurus rules in the natural zodiac, its qualities are intensified here.) You hang onto money for security. You are practical about finances. You feel very deeply about your possessions.

Taurus on the 3ʳᵈ Cusp—You hang onto your ideas for security. You are practical in your thinking. You feel deeply about your ideas.

Taurus on the 4ᵗʰ Cusp—You hang onto your home and family for security. The foundation of your life is based on practicality. You feel very deeply about home, family and security.

Taurus on the 5ᵗʰ Cusp—You hang onto your children for security. You are practical about sex and romance. You feel very deeply about fun.

Taurus on the 6th Cusp—You hang onto your job for security. You are practical at work. You feel very deeply about serving.

Taurus on the 7th Cusp—You hang onto partnership for security. You are practical about marriage. You feel very deeply about partnership.

Taurus on the 8th Cusp—You hang onto your secrets for security. You are practical about psychic matters. You feel deeply about your dreams.

Taurus on the 9th Cusp—You hang onto your philosophy for security. Your philosophy is a practical one. You feel very deeply about God.

Taurus on the 10th Cusp—You hang onto power for security. You are practical about leadership. You feel very deeply about your career.

Taurus on the 11th Cusp—You hang onto friends for security. You are practical about friendship. You feel very deeply about your friends.

Taurus on the 12th Cusp—You hang onto your privacy for security. You are practical about service. You may not be aware how deeply you feel.

♊

Gemini on the Cusps

Gemini teaches the principle of communication. This many-faceted sign gives you curiosity and the ability to see both sides of the picture.

Basic Sentences

You are curious about _____.
There can be a duality in _____.
You talk about _____.

Gemini on the 1ˢᵗ Cusp—You are curious. There can be a duality in your personality. You talk about yourself.

Gemini on the 2ⁿᵈ Cusp—You are curious about finances. There can be a duality in your values. You talk about your possessions.

Gemini on the 3ʳᵈ Cusp—(Since this is the house that Gemini rules in the natural zodiac, its qualities are intensified here.) You are very curious. There can be a duality in the way you think and talk. You TALK.

Gemini on the 4ᵗʰ Cusp—You are curious about your family. There is a duality at the very foundation of your life. You talk about your family.

Gemini on the 5ᵗʰ Cusp—You are curious about children. There can be a duality in your attitude toward fun. You talk about your love life.

Gemini on the 6th Cusp—You are curious about health matters. There can be a duality in the work your do. You talk about your health.

Gemini on the 7th Cusp—You are curious about others. There can be a duality in your approach to marriage. You talk about your spouse.

Gemini on the 8th Cusp—You are curious about the unknown. Your duality will undergo a transformation. You talk about your dreams.

Gemini on the 9th Cusp—You are curious about far away places. Your philosophy is dualistic. You talk about your concepts.

Gemini on the 10th Cusp—You are curious about authority figures. There can be a duality in your public image. You talk about your career.

Gemini on the 11th Cusp—You are curious about groups. There can be a duality in your hopes and wishes. You talk about your friends.

Gemini on the 12th Cusp—You are curious about behind-the-scenes activities. There is a subconscious duality about you. You talk about serving.

ॐ

Cancer on the Cusps

Cancer is a nurturing, protective sign. It represents the need for emotional security.

Basic Sentences

You are protective of _____.
You identify personally with _____.
_____ fulfills your need for emotional security.
You are sensitive and defensive about _____.

Cancer on the 1st Cusp—You are self-protective. You identify personally with yourself, i.e., you can't get away from yourself. You fulfill your need for emotional security. You are sensitive and defensive.

Cancer on the 2nd Cusp—You are protective of your possessions. You identify personally with your possessions. Money fulfills your need for emotional security. You are sensitive and defensive about your possessions.

Cancer on the 3rd Cusp—You are protective of your siblings. You identify personally with your ideas. Talking fulfills your need for emotional security. You are sensitive and defensive about your ideas.

Cancer on the 4th Cusp—(Since this is the house that Cancer rules in the natural zodiac, its qualities are intensified here.) You are protective of your family. You identify personally with your home. Your family fulfills your need for emotional security. You are sensitive and defensive about your home and family.

Cancer on the 5th Cusp—You are protective of your children. You identify personally with your children. Romance fulfills your need for emotional security. You are sensitive and defensive about your children.

Cancer on the 6th Cusp—You are protective of your work. You identify personally with working people. Work fulfills your need for emotional security. You are sensitive and defensive about your job.

Cancer on the 7th Cusp—You are protective of your spouse. You identify personally with other people. Marriage fulfills your need for emotional security. You are sensitive and defensive about your marriage.

Cancer on the 8th Cusp—You are protective of your secrets. You identify personally with your dreams. Other people's money fulfills your need for emotional security. Your sensitivity and defensiveness will undergo a transformation.

Cancer on the 9th Cusp—Your philosophy involves self-protection. You identify personally with your beliefs. Travel fulfills your need for emotional security. You are sensitive and defensive about your beliefs.

Cancer on the 10th Cusp—You are protective of your public image. You identify personally with authority figures. Your career fulfills your need for emotional security. You are sensitive and defensive about your public image.

Cancer on the 11th Cusp—You are protective of your friends. You identify personally with your friends. Friendship fulfills your need for emotional security. You are sensitive and defensive about your friends.

Cancer on the 12ᵗʰ Cusp—You are protective of your private life. You identify personally with those who are confined. Behind-the-scenes service fulfills your need for emotional security. You are unconsciously sensitive and defensive.

♌
Leo on the Cusps

Leo is a proud, creative sign that often loves to be the center of attention—and loves to have fun.

Basic Sentences
You are proud of _____.
You are creative in/with _____.
You want _____ to be the center of attention.
You love to have fun with _____.

Leo on the 1ˢᵗ Cusp—You are proud of yourself. You are creative. You want to be the center of attention. You love to have fun.

Leo on the 2ⁿᵈ Cusp—You are proud of your possessions. You are creative with money. You want your possessions to be the center of attention. You love to have fun with money.

Leo on the 3ʳᵈ Cusp—You are proud of your ideas. You are creative with words. You want your ideas to be the center of attention. You love to have fun with words.

Leo on the 4ᵗʰ Cusp—You are proud of your family. You are creative at home. You want your home to be the center of attention. You love to have fun with your family.

Leo on the 5ᵗʰ Cusp—(Since this is the house that Leo rules in the natural zodiac, its qualities are intensified here.) You are proud of your children. You are creative. You want your children to be the center of attention. You love to have fun with your children.

Leo on the 6ᵗʰ Cusp—You are proud of your employees. You are creative at work. You want your work to be the center of attention. You love to have fun at work.

Leo on the 7ᵗʰ Cusp—You are proud of your spouse. You are creative with others. You want your partner to be the center of attention. You love to have fun with others.

Leo on the 8ᵗʰ Cusp—You are proud of your psychic ability. You are creative with other people's money. Your need to be the center of attention will be transformed. You love to have fun privately.

Leo on the 9ᵗʰ Cusp—You are proud of your principles. You are creative in your beliefs. You want your beliefs to be the center of attention. You love to have fun by traveling.

Leo on the 10ᵗʰ Cusp—You are proud of your public image. You are creative in your career. You want your authority to be the center of attention. You love to have fun in the leadership role.

Leo on the 11ᵗʰ Cusp—You are proud of your friends. You are creative in groups. You want your hopes to be the center of attention. You love to have fun with your friends.

Leo on the 12th Cusp—You are proud of serving behind the scenes. You are creative behind the scenes. Your private world is the center of your attention. You love to have fun behind closed doors.

♍
Virgo on the Cusps

Virgo, the sign of service, is a humble sign that does not seek the limelight, but simply wants to be needed and useful. Often, Virgo is insecure about his own abilities. He is an excellent critic because he is so analytical.

Basic Senences

You want to serve in _____.
You can be insecure about _____.
You are critical of _____.
You can analyze _____.

Virgo on the 1st Cusp—You want to serve. You can be insecure about yourself. You are critical of yourself. You can analyze yourself.

Virgo on the 2nd Cusp—You want to serve in the area of finance. You can be insecure about your income. You are critical of finances. You can analyze money issues.

Virgo on the 3rd Cusp—You want to serve with your ideas. You can be insecure about your ideas. You are critical of ideas. You can analyze your ideas.

Virgo on the 4th Cusp—You want to serve your family. You can be insecure about your home. You are critical of your family. You can analyze your security needs.

Virgo on the 5th Cusp—You want to serve your children. You can be insecure about your creative talents. You are critical of your children. You can analyze your children.

Virgo on the 6th Cusp—(Since this is the house that Virgo rules in the natural zodiac, its qualities are intensified here.) You want to serve. You can be insecure about your health. You are critical of your job. You can analyze your work.

Virgo on the 7th Cusp—You want to serve others. You can be insecure about marriage. You are critical of your partner. You can analyze your spouse.

Virgo on the 8th Cusp—You want to serve others financially. You can be insecure about your ability to help others with their resources. You are critical of other people's values. You can analyze dreams.

Virgo on the 9th Cusp—Your philosophy involves service. You can be insecure about your beliefs. You are critical of higher education. Your philosophy involves analysis.

Virgo on the 10th Cusp—You want to serve in your career. You can be insecure about being in a position of authority. You are critical of those in power. You can analyze in your career.

Virgo on the 11th Cusp—You want to serve your friends. You can be insecure about your friends. You are critical of groups. You can analyze groups.

Virgo on the 12ᵗʰ Cusp—You want to serve behind the scenes. You can be insecure unconsciously. You are inwardly critical. You can analyze the subconscious.

♎

Libra on the Cusps

Charming Libra, the sign of partnership, while looking for balance and harmony, can argue for the opposition in order to present the other side. Libra likes to make things harmonious, but often finds it difficult to live in harmony once it is established.

Basic Sentences

You want balance in _____.
Partnership is important in _____.
You want to be treated as an equal in/at _____.

Libra on the 1ˢᵗ Cusp—You want balance. Partnership is important to you. You want to be treated as an equal.

Libra on the 2ⁿᵈ Cusp—You want balance in your finances. Partnership is important to you in financial matters. You want to be treated as a financial equal.

Libra on the 3ʳᵈ Cusp—You want balance in your ideas. Equality was important to you even as a child. You want your ideas to be treated as equal with everyone else's.

Libra on the 4ᵗʰ Cusp—You want balance in your home.

Partnership is important emotionally. You want to be treated as an equal in your home.

Libra on the 5th Cusp—You want balance in your social life. Partnership is important to you socially. You treat your children as equals.

Libra on the 6th Cusp—You want balance in your work. Partnership is important at work. You want to be treated as an equal at work.

Libra on the 7th Cusp—(Since this is the house that Libra rules in the natural zodiac, its qualities are intensified here.) You want balance in partnership. Marriage is important to you. You want to be treated as an equal by others.

Libra on the 8th Cusp—You want balance in joint financial matters. Your attitude toward partnership will undergo a change. You treat other people's values as equal with your own.

Libra on the 9th Cusp—You want balance in your beliefs. Balance is part of your philosophy. You want your beliefs to be treated as equal with everyone else's.

Libra on the 10th Cusp—You want balance in your career. Partnership is important to you in your career. You want to be treated as an equal in your career.

Libra on the 11th Cusp—You want balance in friendship circles. Partnership is important in fulfilling your hopes and wishes. You want to be treated as an equal by your friends.

Libra on the 12th Cusp—You unconsciously want balance. There may be a private side to your partnerships. Unconsciously, you want to be treated as an equal.

♏

Scorpio on the Cusps

Scorpio, the sign of secrets, deals with the principle of regeneration. Wherever it falls in your chart is the area over which you want to control. However, that is the area which will undergo a change.

Basic Sentences

_____ will undergo a change.
You want to control _____.
You can manipulate _____.
You are secretive about _____.

Scorpio on the 1st Cusp—Your personality will undergo a change. You want to control yourself. You can be manipulative. You are secretive.

Scorpio on the 2nd Cusp—Your values will undergo a change. You want to control your finances. You can manipulate money. You are secretive about your finances.

Scorpio on the 3rd Cusp—Your thinking will undergo a change. You want to control your ideas. You can manipulate with words. You are secretive about your thoughts.

Scorpio on the 4th Cusp—Your emotional security needs will undergo a change. You want to control your family. You can manipulate your family. You are secretive about your home and family.

Scorpio on the 5th Cusp—Your creativity will undergo a change. You want to control your children. You can manipulate social situations. You are secretive about your fun.

Scorpio on the 6th Cusp—Your work will undergo a change. You want to control your work. You can manipulate at work. You are secretive about your job.

Scorpio on the 7th Cusp—Your partnership will undergo a change. You want to control your spouse. You can manipulate others. You are secretive about your partnerships.

Scorpio on the 8th Cusp—(Since this is the house that Scorpio rules in the natural zodiac, its qualities are intensified here.) Your need for control will undergo a change. You want to control other people's values. You can manipulate psychically. You are very secretive.

Scorpio on the 9th Cusp—Your beliefs will change. Your philosophy involves control. You believe in manipulation. You are secretive about your beliefs.

Scorpio on the 10th Cusp—Your career will undergo a change. You want to control your career. You can manipulate in your career. You are secretive about your career.

Scorpio on the 11th Cusp—Your hopes and wishes will undergo a change. You want to control your friends. You can manipulate groups. You are secretive about friendship.

Scorpio on the 12th Cusp—Your subconscious need for control will change. You control behind the scenes. You may not be aware of your ability to manipulate. You are secretive about your private life.

♐
Sagittarius on the Cusps

Sagittarius deals with expansion on all levels. He is generous and philosophical about life, and wants to be free to live according to his principles. He is honest and tells the truth—but he exaggerates for effect.

Basic Sentences
You are philosophical about _____.
You are honest and generous in/with _____.
You exaggerate _____.

Sagittarius on the 1st Cusp—You are philosophical. You are honest and generous. You exaggerate.

Sagittarius on the 2nd Cusp—You are philosophical about money. You are honest and generous with money. You exaggerate your finances.

Sagittarius on the 3rd Cusp—Your thinking is philosophical. You are honest in what you say and generous with your ideas. Your exaggerate when you speak.

Sagittarius on the 4th Cusp—You are philosophical about your family. You are honest and generous with family members. You exaggerate your emotional security needs.

Sagittarius on the 5th Cusp—You are philosophical about your social life. You are honest and generous with children. You exaggerate your talents.

Sagittarius on the 6th Cusp—You are philosophical about work. You are honest and generous at work. You exaggerate your job.

Sagittarius on the 7th Cusp—You are philosophical about marriage. You are honest and generous with others. You exaggerate with your partner.

Sagittarius on the 8th Cusp—You are philosophical about joint finances. You are honest and generous in joint financial matters. Your tendency to exaggerate will undergo a change.

Sagittarius on the 9th Cusp—(Since this is the house that Sagittarius rules in the natural zodiac, its qualities are intensified here.) You are very philosophical. Your beliefs include honesty and generosity. You exaggerate your beliefs.

Sagittarius on the 10th Cusp—You are philosophical about power. You are honest and generous in your career. You can exaggerate your power and authority.

Sagittarius on the 11th Cusp—You are philosophical about friendship. You are honest and generous with your friends. You exaggerate with friends.

Sagittarius on the 12th Cusp—You are philosophical about spiritual service. You are privately honest and generous. You can exaggerate without realizing it.

♑
Capricorn on the Cusps

Capricorn is traditional and believes in reward for hard work. Capricorn's goal is to be in a position of authority and respect.

Basic Sentences

You want to be respected and powerful in/with _____.
You are conservative and traditional in/with _____.
You accept responsibility in/with _____.

Capricorn on the 1ˢᵗ Cusp—You want to be respected and powerful. You are conservative and traditional. You accept responsibility.

Capricorn on the 2ⁿᵈ Cusp—You want to be respected and powerful financially. You are conservative and traditional with money. You accept financial responsibility.

Capricorn on the 3ʳᵈ Cusp—You want your ideas to be respected and powerful. Your thinking is conservative and traditional. You accepted your responsibility as a child.

Capricorn on the 4ᵗʰ Cusp—You want to be respected and powerful in your home. You are conservative and traditional in your need for security. Accept your responsibility with your family.

Capricorn on the 5ᵗʰ Cusp—You want to be respected and powerful with children. You are conservative and traditional when it comes to fun. You accept your responsibility with your children.

Capricorn on the 6th Cusp—You want to be respected and powerful at work. You are conservative and traditional in your approach to health matters. You accept your responsibility at work.

Capricorn on the 7th Cusp—You want to be respected and powerful in partnership. You are conservative and traditional when it comes to marriage. You accept your responsibility with others.

Capricorn on the 8th Cusp—Your need for respect and power will change. You are conservative and traditional with other people's money. You accept your responsibility in joint financial ventures.

Capricorn on the 9th Cusp—Respect and power are part of your belief system. You are conservative and traditional in your approach to God. Your philosophy of life involves accepting responsibility.

Capricorn on the 10th Cusp—(Since this is the house that Capricorn rules in the natural zodiac, its qualities are intensified here.) You want to be respected and powerful in your career. You are conservative and traditional in your approach to authority. You accept your responsibility as a leader.

Capricorn on the 11th Cusp—You want to be respected and powerful with groups. You are conservative and traditional in your approach to friends. You accept your responsibility as a friend.

Capricorn on the 12th Cusp—You have an unconscious need to be respected and powerful. You are, unknowingly, conservative and traditional. You accept your responsibility in private matters.

♒
Aquarius on the Cusps

Aquarius often feels like an alien because, while he likes people, he does not necessarily need them. He is a loner, but he's not lonely. He marches to his own drumbeat, uninfluenced by others.

Basic Sentences

You are your own person in/with _____.
Your _____ is/are ahead of the times.
You are both traditional and original in/with _____.

Aquarius on the 1ˢᵗ Cusp—You are your own person. You are ahead of the times. You are both traditional and original.

Aquarius on the 2ⁿᵈ Cusp—You are your own person financially. Your values are ahead of the times. You are both traditional and original with money.

Aquarius on the 3ʳᵈ Cusp—You are your own person in your thinking. Your ideas are ahead of the times. Your thinking is both traditional and original.

Aquarius on the 4ᵗʰ Cusp—You are your own person with your family. Your home is ahead of the times. You are both traditional and original with your family.

Aquarius on the 5ᵗʰ Cusp—You are your own person when you have fun. Your creations are ahead of the times. You are both traditional and original with children.

Aquarius on the 6ᵗʰ Cusp—You are your own person at work. Your job is ahead of the times. You are both traditional and original in health matters.

Aquarius on the 7ᵗʰ Cusp—You are your own person in partnership. Your dealings with others are ahead of the times. You are both traditional and original in your marriage.

Aquarius on the 8ᵗʰ Cusp—You are your own person in psychic matters. Your intuition is ahead of the times. You are both traditional and original in joint financial matters.

Aquarius on the 9ᵗʰ Cusp—Your philosophy involves being your own person. Your beliefs are ahead of the times. Your principles are both traditional and original.

Aquarius on the 10ᵗʰ Cusp—You are your own person in your career. Your leadership style is ahead of the times. You are both traditional and conservative as a leader.

Aquarius on the 11ᵗʰ Cusp—(Since this is the house that Aquarius rules in the natural zodiac, its qualities are intensified here.) You are your own person in groups. Your hopes and wishes are ahead of the times. Your friends are both traditional and original.

Aquarius on the 12ᵗʰ Cusp—You are your own person in private. You are ahead of the times in spiritual service. Subconsciously, you are both traditional and original.

♓
Pisces on the Cusps

Pisces can function on the highest of spiritual levels or avoid reality through day-dreaming, escape, and self-indulgence. Pisces is looking for something greater than himself to serve.

Basic Sentences

You can either serve _____ or escape from responsibility.
You are either idealistic about or inspired by _____.
You can be undecided about _____.

Pisces on the 1ˢᵗ Cusp—You can either serve or escape from life. You are either idealistic or inspired. You can be undecided.

Pisces on the 2ⁿᵈ Cusp—You can either serve financially or escape from financial responsibility. You are either idealistic about or inspired by money. You can be undecided about your values.

Pisces on the 3ʳᵈ Cusp—You either served or escaped from reality in childhood. You are either idealistic or inspired in your thinking. You can be undecided in your thinking.

Pisces on the 4ᵗʰ Cusp—You can either serve your family or escape from family responsibility. You are either idealistic about or inspired by your family. You can be undecided about your family role.

Pisces on the 5ᵗʰ Cusp—You can either serve your children or escape into fun and games. You are either idealistic about or inspired by children. You can be undecided about your love life.

Pisces on the 6ᵗʰ Cusp—You can either serve at work or escape from responsibility. You are either idealistic about or inspired by your job. You can be undecided about health matters.

Pisces on the 7ᵗʰ Cusp—You can either serve your partner or escape from responsibility. You are either idealistic about or inspired by marriage. You can be undecided about partnership matters.

Pisces on the 8ᵗʰ Cusp—You can either serve others by inspiring them about their values or escape into dreams. Idealism and wishful thinking will be transformed into inspiration. Indecision will be transformed into inspiration.

Pisces on the 9ᵗʰ Cusp—Your philosophy involves either serving or escaping. Your beliefs are either idealistic or inspired. You can be undecided about what you believe.

Pisces on the 10ᵗʰ Cusp—You can either serve as a leader or escape from responsibility. You are either idealistic about or inspired by those in authority. You can be undecided about your career.

Pisces on the 11ᵗʰ Cusp—You can either serve the groups to which you belong or escape from responsibility. You are either idealistic about or inspired by your friends. You can be undecided about your hopes and wishes.

Pisces on the 12ᵗʰ Cusp—(Since this is the house that Pisces rules in the natural zodiac, its qualities are intensified here.) You can either serve behind the scenes or escape there. You are either idealistic or inspired. You may be unconsciously undecided.

PLANETS IN THE HOUSES

PLANETS ARE THE ROVING DELEGATES or representatives of the signs. They illustrate the principles to be learned. The sign in which a planet falls tells us HOW we will learn the principle it represents; the house in which it falls tells us the area of life (WHERE) we will learn the principle, and the aspects between planets tell us whether we will learn all this with ease or difficulty. The BASIC SENTENCE approach is the easiest way to understand what the planets are showing us by their house placement. Compose a few BASIC SENTENCES to describe each planet, then apply them to the house in which the planet falls. As with all

BASIC SENTENCES, some may need to be modified to fit. Remember that these sentences are suggestions and should be used as a starting point.

☉
The Sun

The Sun, called "the Giver of Life", is the center of our solar system. The Sun rules our individuality, our ego. It rules the creative urge—and pride in what we have created. The Sun represents the "positive", aggressive or masculine principle, and, consequently, the father or other male authority figures in our lives.

Basic Sentences

You are proud of _____.
_____ is the center of your life.
You are creative in/with _____.
You express your individuality in/with _____.
You express your authority in/with _____.

Sun in the 1ˢᵗ House: You are proud of yourself. You are the center of your life. You are creative. You express your individuality through your personality and appearance. You express your authority through your personality.

Sun in the 2ⁿᵈ House: You are proud of your possessions. Money is the center of your life. You are creative with finances. You express your individuality through your possessions. You express your authority with money.

Sun in the 3ʳᵈ House: You are proud of your ideas. Communication is the center of your life. You are creative with words. You express your individuality through your ideas. You express your authority with words.

Sun in the 4th House: You are proud of your home. Your family is the center of your life. You are creative with your family. You express your individuality in your home. You express your authority with your family.

Sun in the 5th House: (Because of Leo's rulership of the natural 5th house, the Sun is extremely strong here.) You are proud of what you create. Your children are the center of your life. You are very creative. You express your individuality in romantic/ fun settings. You express your authority dramatically.

Sun in the 6th House: You are proud of your health. Your work is the center of your life. You are creative at work. You express your individuality at work. You express your authority with your employees.

Sun in the 7th House: You are proud of your partner. (However, since this is your partner's 1st house, your partner is proud of himself.) Other people are the center of your life. You are creative in partnership. You express your individuality with your spouse. You express your authority with others.

Sun in the 8th House: You are proud of your psychic ability. Control is the center of your life. You are creative with other people's resources. You express your individuality psychically. You express your authority by empowering others to develop their talents and resources.

Sun in the 9th House: You are proud of your philosophy. Your principles are the center of your life. Your philosophy involves being creative. You express your individuality in your beliefs. Your philosophy involves expressing your authority.

Sun in the 10ᵗʰ House: You are proud of your authority. Power is the center of your life. You are creative in your career. You express your individuality from a position of power. You express your authority in your career.

Sun in the 11ᵗʰ House: You are proud of your friends. Friendship is the center of your life. You are creative in groups. You express your individuality in groups. You express your authority with your friends.

Sun in the 12ᵗʰ House: You are proud of your faith. Privacy is the center of your life. You are creative behind the scenes. You express your individuality through service. You express your authority behind-the-scenes.

☽
The Moon

The Moon is the "negative", receptive or feminine principle in each of us and represents the females in our lives, especially the mother. Because of this, the Moon governs the protective urge. The Moon is changeable and rules our emotions and moods. On a large scale, it rules the public. Just as we look to our mother for our emotional security, so the Moon shows us where we look to find the fulfillment of this need. The Moon represents the personality. Because it deals with what we have brought over from the past, it rules the subconscious. The Moon also relates to our health because it rules function and form, the ebb and flow of life.

Basic Sentences

There are changes in _____.
You are emotional about _____.
You are protective of _____.
Your mother influences _____.
You look to _____ for emotional security.

Moon in the 1st House: There are changes in your personality. You are emotional. You are self-protective. Your mother influences your personality. You look to yourself for emotional security.

Moon in the 2nd House: There are changes in your values. You are emotional about money. You are protective of your possessions. Your mother influences your values. You look to money for emotional security.

Moon in the 3rd House: There are changes in your thinking. Your thinking is emotional. You are protective of your ideas. Your mother influences your self-expression. You talk to fulfill your emotional security needs.

Moon in the 4th House: (The Moon is stronger here due to Cancer's rulership of the natural 4th house.) There are changes in your home. You are emotional about your family. You are protective of your home and family. Your mother influences your emotional security needs. You look to your mother for emotional security.

Moon in the 5th House: There are changes in your social life. You are emotional about your children. You are protective of anything you create. Your mother influences your attitude toward fun. You look to your children for emotional security.

Moon in the 6ᵗʰ House: There are changes in your job. You are emotional about your health. You are protective of your work. Your mother influences your health. You look to your job for emotional security.

Moon in the 7ᵗʰ House: There are changes in your partnerships. You are emotional about marriage. You are protective of others. Your mother influences your attitude toward marriage. You look to others for emotional security.

Moon in the 8ᵗʰ House: There are changes in your psychic awareness. You are emotional about being in control. You are protective of your secrets. Your attitude toward your mother will undergo a total change. Your emotional security needs will be transformed.

Moon in the 9ᵗʰ House: There are changes in your attitude toward God. You are emotional about your beliefs. You are protective of your principles. Your mother influences your philosophy of life. You look to God for emotional security.

Moon in the 10ᵗʰ House: There are changes in your career. You are emotional about your reputation. You are protective of your public image. Your mother influences your career. You look to your career for emotional security.

Moon in the 11ᵗʰ House: There are changes in your hopes and wishes. You are emotional about your friends. You are protective of your friends. Your mother influences your hopes and wishes. You look to your friends for emotional security.

Moon in the 12ᵗʰ House: There are subconscious emotional changes. You are emotional about service. You are protective of your privacy. Your mother's influence is hidden. You look to solitude for emotional security.

☿
Mercury

Mercury takes the instinctive, emotional, subconscious reaction of the Moon and brings it to consciousness. Mercury is our communicator, whether from subconscious to conscious or from person to person. Mercury does not necessarily come up with the idea—Mercury puts it into words. It rules communication, correspondence, short distance travel and siblings.

Basic Sentence
You think and talk about _____.

Mercury in the 1ˢᵗ House: You think and talk about yourself.

Mercury in the 2ⁿᵈ House: You think and talk about money.

Mercury in the 3ʳᵈ House: (Mercury is stronger here due to Gemini's rulership of the natural 3ʳᵈ house.) You think and talk a lot.

Mercury in the 4ᵗʰ House: You think and talk about your home, family and security.

Mercury in the 5ᵗʰ House: You think and talk about your children.

Mercury in the 6ᵗʰ House: (Mercury is stronger here due to Virgo's rulership of the natural 6ᵗʰ house.) You think and talk about your work.

Mercury in the 7ᵗʰ House: You think and talk about your spouse, but since this is your spouse's 1ˢᵗ house, he thinks and talks about himself.

Mercury in the 8ᵗʰ House: You think and talk about the secrets of life. Your thinking will be transformed.

Mercury in the 9ᵗʰ House: You think and talk about your beliefs.

Mercury in the 10ᵗʰ House: You think and talk about your career.

Mercury in the 11ᵗʰ House: You think and talk about your friends.

Mercury in the 12ᵗʰ House: Your thoughts are private.

♀
Venus

Venus, the Lesser Benefic, is the principle of love, beauty and harmony. It rules our social desires and all the pleasures of life.

Basic Sentences
_____ *is beautiful to you.*
You love _____.

Venus in the 1ˢᵗ House: You are beautiful. You love yourself.

Venus in the 2ⁿᵈ House: (Venus is stronger here due to Taurus's rulership of the natural 2ⁿᵈ house.) Your possessions are beautiful to you. You love money.

Venus in the 3ʳᵈ House: Your ideas are beautiful to you. You love to talk.

Venus in the 4ᵗʰ House: Your home is beautiful to you. You love your family.

Venus in the 5ᵗʰ House: Romance is beautiful to you. You love your children.

Venus in the 6ᵗʰ House: Service is beautiful to you. You love your work.

Venus in the 7ᵗʰ House: (Venus is stronger here due to Libra's rulership of the natural 7ᵗʰ house.) Your spouse is beautiful to you—and to himself, since your 7ᵗʰ is his 1ˢᵗ. You love partnership.

Venus in the 8ᵗʰ House: Your concept of love and beauty will be transformed. You love secrets.

Venus in the 9ᵗʰ House: Your philosophy involves love and beauty. You love to travel.

Venus in the 10ᵗʰ House: Your public image is beautiful to you. You love being the leader.

Venus in the 11ᵗʰ House: Friendship is beautiful to you. You love group activities.

Venus in the 12ᵗʰ House: Spiritual service is beautiful to you. You love solitude.

♂
Mars

Mars is the principle of energy and action. Mars is the opposite of Venus. Venus is love; Mars is passion (sex). Venus rules the social urges; Mars rules the personal desires. Venus is passive; Mars is active. Venus is love; Mars is hate. Venus is peace and conciliation; Mars is strife and war. Venus rules rhythm and harmony; Mars is impulsive. Venus rules the arts; Mars rules sports. Mars, along with the Sun, is the co-significator of the young men in our lives.

Basic Sentences

You resent/hate _____.
You are aggressive in/with _____.
You throw yourself into _____.
_____ comes first.
You will fight for or with _____.

Mars in the 1ˢᵗ House: (Mars is stronger here due to Aries' rulership of the natural 1ˢᵗ house.) You hate yourself. You are aggressive. You throw yourself into whatever you want. You come first. You will fight for or with yourself.

Mars in the 2ⁿᵈ House: You hate not having money. You are financially aggressive. You throw yourself into making money. Money comes first. You will fight for or with money.

Mars in the 3ʳᵈ House: You resent something about your

childhood. You speak aggressively. You throw yourself into your ideas. Your ideas come first. You will fight for or with your ideas.

Mars in the 4th House: You resent your family. You are aggressive at home. You throw yourself into fulfilling your security needs. Your family comes first. You will fight for or with your family.

Mars in the 5th House: You resent your children. You are sexually aggressive. You throw yourself into fun and games. Your love life comes first. You will fight for or with your children.

Mars in the 6th House: You resent working. You are aggressive in your work. You throw yourself into your work. Your work comes first. You will fight for or with your employees.

Mars in the 7th House: You resent your spouse. You are aggressive in partnership. You throw yourself into relationships. Your spouse comes first, but since your 7th house is his 1st house, he comes first to himself.

Mars in the 8th House: (Mars is stronger here due to Scorpio's rulership of the natural 8th house.) You have hidden anger, which will be transformed. You are aggressive, but it may be hidden. You throw yourself into positions of control. Secrets come first to you. You will fight for or with other people's resources.

Mars in the 9th House: Your philosophy involves resentment. You are aggressive when it comes to your beliefs. You throw yourself into your beliefs. Your principles come first. You will fight for or with your principles.

Mars in the 10ᵗʰ House: You resent authority figures. You are aggressive when it comes to assuming authority. You throw yourself into leadership positions. Your career comes first. You will fight for or with authority figures.

Mars in the 11ᵗʰ House: You resent groups. You are aggressive in groups. You throw yourself into friendship. Your hopes and wishes come first. You will fight for or with friends.

Mars in the 12ᵗʰ House: You have hidden anger. You are aggressive behind the scenes. You throw yourself into private service. Your privacy comes first. Subconsciously, you are a fighter.

♃

Jupiter

Jupiter, the Great Benefic, is the planet of reward, giving us abundance, happiness, optimism and friendship. Jupiter teaches us the principles of God's law, and blesses us wherever it falls in our chart. It is the planet of luck, and rules money, philosophy, long trips, legal affairs and the higher mind.

Basic Sentences

You are lucky in/with _____.
You have a lot of _____.
You are generous with _____.
You believe in _____.

Jupiter in the 1ˢᵗ House: You are lucky. You have a lot of personality. You are generous. You believe in yourself.

Jupiter in the 2nd House: You are lucky with money. You have many possessions. You are generous with your money. You believe in money.

Jupiter in the 3rd House: You were lucky in childhood. You have a lot to say. You are generous with your ideas. You believe in your ideas.

Jupiter in the 4th House: You are lucky with real estate. You have a lot of security. You are generous with your family. You believe in your family.

Jupiter in the 5th House: You are lucky in romance. You have a lot of fun. You are generous with your children. You believe in children.

Jupiter in the 6th House: You are lucky in health matters. You have a lot of work. You are generous with employees. You believe in work and service.

Jupiter in the 7th House: You are lucky in marriage. You have many partners. You are generous with others. You believe in partnership.

Jupiter in the 8th House: You are lucky with other people's money. You have a lot of psychic power. You are generous in joint financial matters. Your beliefs will undergo a change.

Jupiter in the 9th House: (Jupiter is stronger here due to Sagittarius' rulership of the natural 9th house.) You are lucky in your travels, either in or out of the body. You have many opportunities to expand your horizons. Your philosophy is one of generosity. You believe in God.

Jupiter in the 10ᵗʰ House: You are lucky in your career. You have a lot of authority. You are a generous leader. You believe in your leadership ability.

Jupiter in the 11ᵗʰ House: You are lucky in friendship. You have a lot of friends. You are generous with your friends. You believe in friendship.

Jupiter in the 12ᵗʰ House: (Jupiter is stronger here due to Pisces' rulership of the natural 12ᵗʰ house.) You have hidden luck. You have a lot of faith. You are very generous. You believe in spiritual fulfillment through service to God.

♄
Saturn

Saturn is the polar opposite of Jupiter. Jupiter is expansion; Saturn is contraction. Jupiter is law; Saturn is order. Jupiter is God's law; Saturn is man's (society's) law. Jupiter is freedom; Saturn is discipline, restriction. Jupiter is abundance; Saturn is limitation. Jupiter is wealth; Saturn is financial restriction. Jupiter is optimism; Saturn is seriousness. Jupiter is impulsive; Saturn is disciplined. Jupiter is outgoing; Saturn is reserved. Jupiter is idealization; Saturn is wisdom through experience. Jupiter rewards; Saturn tests. Saturn is the principle of crystallization and the test in the use of power. Saturn rules time and the lessons time teaches. Saturn is responsibility, i.e., responding to your ability. Saturn rules the earth and real estate, old people and things, and falls. Saturn rules fear, and tells us that by looking realistically at what we fear, we can overcome it.

Basic Sentences

You are either afraid of _____ responsibility or you accept it.
You feel restricted in _____.
You are serious about _____.
You assert your authority in/by/with _____.
You are traditional with/about _____.

Saturn in the 1st House: You are either afraid of taking your responsibility or you accept it. You feel personal restrictions. You are serious. You assert your authority. You are traditional.

Saturn in the 2nd House: You are either afraid of financial responsibility or you accept it. You feel restricted financially. You are serious about money. You assert your authority financially. You are traditional about money.

Saturn in the 3rd House: You are either afraid of expressing your ideas or you take your responsibility and speak up. You feel restricted in self-expression. You are serious about your ideas. You assert your authority with your siblings. You are traditional in your thinking.

Saturn in the 4th House: You are either afraid of the responsibility of a family or you accept it. You feel restricted at home. You are serious about your family. You assert your authority at home. You are traditional about home and family.

Saturn in the 5th House: You are either afraid of the responsibility of children or you accept it. You feel restricted by children. You are serious about romance. You assert your authority with your children. You are traditional about fun.

Saturn in the 6th House: You are either afraid of taking your responsibility at work or you accept it. You feel restricted at work. You are serious about health matters. You assert your authority at work. You are traditional in your attitude toward work and service.

Saturn in the 7th House: You are either afraid of the responsibility of marriage, or you accept it. You feel restricted in partnership. You are serious about partnership. You assert your authority with others. You are traditional when it comes to marriage.

Saturn in the 8th House: Your fear of the unknown will be transformed. You feel restricted in joint financial matters. You are serious about your dreams. Your concept of authority and power will undergo a change. You are traditional about other people's values.

Saturn in the 9th House: You are either afraid of God or have taken responsibility for your beliefs. You feel restricted when it comes to higher education. You are serious about your principles. Your philosophy involves asserting your authority. You are traditional in your beliefs about God.

Saturn in the 10th House: (Saturn is stronger here due to Capricorn's rulership of the natural 10th house.) You are either afraid of leadership or have taken your responsibility as a leader. You feel restricted in by leadership. You are serious about your career. You assert your authority in your career. You are traditional in your attitude toward power and leadership.

Saturn in the 11th House: (Saturn is stronger here due to

Aquarius' rulership of the natural 11th house.) You are either afraid of groups or have taken your responsibility with them. You feel restricted by groups. You are serious about friendship. You assert your authority in groups. You are traditional when it comes to friendship.

Saturn in the 12th House: You are either afraid of the unknown or have taken responsibility to face your fears. Unknowingly, you feel restricted. You take your private life seriously. You assert your authority behind the scenes. There is a hidden element of tradition which motivates you.

⛢

Uranus

Uranus is the Awakener and shatters the crystallization of Saturn by breaking up old habit patterns. Instead of following the rules of order set down by Saturn, Uranus expresses individuality and inventiveness. Saturn does things slowly; Uranus acts suddenly and unexpectedly. Saturn asks, "Why?"; Uranus asks, "Why not?" Saturn rules the old; Uranus rules the new. It rules electricity, intuition, invention, psychic ability, machinery and astrology.

Basic Sentences
Your _____ is unpredictable.
You are original and inventive in/with _____.
You can be self-willed and rebellious in/with _____.

Uranus in the 1st House: You are unpredictable. You are original and inventive. You can be self-willed and rebellious.

Uranus in the 2nd House: Your finances are unpredictable. You are original and inventive with money. You can be self-willed and rebellious financially.

Uranus in the 3rd House: Your ideas are unpredictable. You are original and inventive in your thinking. You were probably self-willed and rebellious as a child.

Uranus in the 4th House: Your home life is unpredictable. You are original and inventive in your home. You can be self-willed and rebellious with your family.

Uranus in the 5th House: Your children are unpredictable. You are original and inventive sexually. You can be self-willed and rebellious in social situations.

Uranus in the 6th House: Your health is unpredictable. You are original and inventive in your work. You can be self-willed at work.

Uranus in the 7th House: Your partnerships are unpredictable. You are original and inventive with others. You can be self-willed and rebellious in marriage.

Uranus in the 8th House: Your unpredictability will be transformed. You are original and inventive psychically. Your self-will and rebellion will undergo a change.

Uranus in the 9th House: Your philosophy involves being unpredictable. You are original and inventive in your beliefs. Your philosophy can include self-will and rebellion.

Uranus in the 10th House: Your career is unpredictable. You are original and inventive in your career. You can be self-willed and rebellious as a leader.

Uranus in the 11ᵗʰ House: (Uranus is stronger here due to Aquarius' rulership of the natural 11ᵗʰ house.) Your goals are unpredictable. You are original and inventive in groups. You can be self-willed and rebellious with friends.

Uranus in the 12ᵗʰ House: Your private life is unpredictable. You are original and inventive in private. Your self-will and rebellion are hidden.

Ψ
Neptune

Comparing Neptune with Saturn will help define Neptune. The crystallization of Saturn is dissolved by the spirituality of Neptune, just as the restriction of the earth plane is dissolved through a oneness with God. Trying to describe Neptune is like trying to grab a handful of smoke. Saturn's vibration is heavy; Neptune's is tenuous. Saturn is practical; Neptune is dreamy and idealistic. Saturn deals with reality; Neptune deals with inspiration. Saturn is the earth plane; Neptune is the spirit plane. Saturn builds; Neptune dissolves. Wherever Neptune falls in our chart is where we are looking for Divine Perfection and the fulfillment of your dream. Sometimes in our search for our dream, we lose sight of reality (Saturn). Neptune can inspire us to follow our dream or it can cloud our vision and deceive us so that we lose sight of our goal. Neptune can express itself as selfless service, or sacrifice and martyrdom. It can trigger indulgent "escapes" of all sorts, i.e., make believe, fantasy, wishful thinking, day-dreaming, sleeping, smoking, drinking, sexual indulgences, etc. Neptune rules divine inspiration, the spirit world, altruistic service, liquids, gases and smoke.

Basic Sentences

You are idealistic about/in _____.
You are either confused or inspired by _____.
You may sacrifice _____.
You may want to escape into _____.

Neptune in the 1ˢᵗ House: You are idealistic about yourself. You are either confused or inspired. You may sacrifice yourself. You may want to escape.

Neptune in the 2ⁿᵈ House: You are idealistic about money. You are either confused or inspired financially. You may sacrifice financially. You may want to escape into your possessions.

Neptune in the 3ʳᵈ House: You are idealistic in your thinking. Your ideas are either confused or inspired. You may have had to sacrifice something in your childhood. You may want to escape into wishful thinking.

Neptune in the 4ᵗʰ House: You are idealistic about your home and family. You are either confused or inspired by your family. You may sacrifice your security. You may want to escape into your home.

Neptune in the 5ᵗʰ House: You are idealistic about romance. You are either confused or inspired by children. You may sacrifice romance. You may want to escape into creative projects.

Neptune in the 6ᵗʰ House: You are idealistic about your

work. You are either confused or inspired by your work. You may have to sacrifice at work. You may want to escape into your work.

Neptune in the 7th House: You are idealistic about partnership. You are either confused or inspired by others. You may have to sacrifice in marriage. You may want to escape into marriage.

Neptune in the 8th House: You ideals will undergo a change. You are either confused or inspired by your dreams. You may sacrifice an inheritance. You may want to escape into your dreams.

Neptune in the 9th House: You are idealistic about God. Your philosophy is either confused or inspired. Your beliefs involve sacrifice. You may want to escape into travel.

Neptune in the 10th House: You are idealistic about your career. You are either confused or inspired by authority figures. You may have to sacrifice in your career. You may want to escape into your career.

Neptune in the 11th House: You are idealistic about your friends. You are either confused or inspired by your friends. You may have to sacrifice in friendship. You may want to escape into group activities.

Neptune in the 12th House: (Neptune is stronger here due to Pisces' rulership of the natural 12th house.) You are idealistic about service. You are either confused or inspired. You may sacrifice through service. You may want to escape into your own private world.

Pluto

Pluto is the principle of transmutation, and brings total upheaval. It rules the cycle of death and rebirth. Pluto is the planet of Frozen Fire, and rules television, atomic energy, undercover activities, mass movements, archeology, psychic perception and extremes in anything. Pluto is the planet of control and manipulation. It represents desire in its most intense form, and is the love/hate principle in action.

Basic Sentences

There are total changes in _____.
You want to be in control of_____.
You are intense about _____.
You both love and hate _____.

Pluto in the 1ˢᵗ House: There are total changes in you and your personality. You want to be in control of yourself. You are intense. You both love and hate yourself.

Pluto in the 2ⁿᵈ House: There are total changes in your values. You want to be in control of your money. Your desires are intense. You both love and hate money.

Pluto in the 3ʳᵈ House: There may have been total changes in your childhood. You want to be in control of your mind. Your ideas are intense. You both love and hate your siblings.

Pluto in the 4ᵗʰ House: There are total changes in your home. You want to be in control of your home and family. You are intense about your security needs. You both love and hate your family.

Pluto in the 5th House: There are total changes in your attitude toward children. You want to be in control of your children. You are intense about sex and romance. You both love and hate your children.

Pluto in the 6th House: There are total changes in your work. You want to be in control of your work and health. You are intense about your work. You both love and hate your work.

Pluto in the 7th House: There are total changes in your partnerships. You want to be in control of your spouse. You are intense about partnership. You both love and hate your spouse.

Pluto in the 8th House: (Pluto is stronger here due to Scorpio's rulership of the natural 8th house.) There are total changes on deep, emotional levels. Your desire for control will undergo a transformation. You are very intense. You will work through and transform your conflicting emotions of love and hate.

Pluto in the 9th House: There are total changes in your philosophy. Your philosophy involves being in control. You are intense about your beliefs. Your philosophy includes strong feelings of both love and hate.

Pluto in the 10th House: There are total changes in your career. You want to be in control of your career. You are intense about your career. You both love and hate being in a position of authority.

Pluto in the 11th House: There are total changes in your hopes and wishes. You want to be in control in groups. You are intense about friendship. You both love and hate your friends.

Pluto in the 12th House: There are total changes that go on behind the scenes. You want to be in control behind the scenes. There is a hidden intensity about you. You are motivated by subconscious feelings of both love and hate.

PLANETS IN THE SIGNS

THE PLANETS REPRESENT PRINCIPLES to be learned. The sign in which a planet falls tells us HOW (in what manner) we will learn that principle. In other words, the planet expresses itself through the sign and seems to take on the sign's personality. A simple way to interpret the planets in the signs is to think of the planet in question as being conjunct the ruler of the sign in question, and then compose a BASIC SENTENCE linking the two. For example, Venus in Aries. Venus rules love, beauty and pleasure. Mars rules energy, action and passion. BASIC SENTENCE: Your love nature is very passionate.

These planets rule the sign they are in and are, therefore, stronger there.

♈

Aries

☉ **Sun in Aries:** Your ego expresses itself in a "me first" way.

☽ **Moon in Aries:** Your moods and emotions are impulsive.

☿ **Mercury in Aries:** You think aggressively.

♀ **Venus in Aries:** You express your love in a very direct manner.

♂ ***Mars in Aries:** You express your energies aggressively.

♃ **Jupiter in Aries:** Your generosity expresses itself impulsively.

♄ **Saturn in Aries:** You express your authority in a "me first" manner.

♅ **Uranus in Aries:** You are explosive and unpredictable.

♆ **Neptune in Aries:** You are torn between escape and action.

♇ **Pluto in Aries:** You control your "me first" nature.

♉

Taurus

☉ **Sun in Taurus:** Your ego is very determined.

☽ **Moon in Taurus:** Your moods are deep and strong.

☿ **Mercury in Taurus:** Your ideas are practical.

♀ ***Venus in Taurus:** Your love nature is very tenacious.

♂ **Mars in Taurus:** Your energies are directed and practical.

♃ **Jupiter in Taurus:** You are loving in friendship.

♄ **Saturn in Taurus:** Your attitude toward authority is practical.

♅ **Uranus in Taurus:** Your inventiveness expresses itself practically.

♆ **Neptune in Taurus:** Your inspiration expresses itself practically.

♇ **Pluto in Taurus:** You control your appetites.

♊

Gemini

☉ **Sun in Gemini:** Your ego expresses itself verbally.

☽ **Moon in Gemini:** Your moods are dualistic.

☿ ***Mercury in Gemini:** Your mind is restless.

♀ **Venus in Gemini:**   You love to talk.

♂ **Mars in Gemini:**   You express your anger verbally.

♃ **Jupiter in Gemini:**   You are generous with ideas.

♄ **Saturn in Gemini:**   You have mental discipline.

♅ **Uranus in Gemini:**   You express your uniqueness verbally.

♆ **Neptune in Gemini:**   You dream of expressing yourself.

♇ **Pluto in Gemini:**   You transform on two levels.

♋

Cancer

☉ **Sun in Cancer:**   Your ego is very self-protective.

☽ ***Moon in Cancer:**   Your moods are very strong and self-protective.

☿ **Mercury in Cancer:** Your thoughts are emotional.

♀ **Venus in Cancer:**   Your love nature is nurturing.

♂ **Mars in Cancer:**   Your energies are aimed at self-protection.

♃ **Jupiter in Cancer:**   Your friendship is maternal.

♄ **Saturn in Cancer:** Your sense of responsibility has emotional overtones.

♅ **Uranus in Cancer:** Your non-conformity is self-protective.

♆ **Neptune in Cancer:** Your dreams are emotional.

♇ **Pluto in Cancer:** Your security needs undergo a transformation.

♌
Leo

☉ ***Sun in Leo:** Your ego expresses itself dramatically.

☽ **Moon in Leo:** You express your moods dramatically.

☿ **Mercury in Leo:** Your mind is very creative.

♀ **Venus in Leo:** You love to have fun.

♂ **Mars in Leo:** Your energies are creative.

♃ **Jupiter in Leo:** You express your generosity dramatically.

♄ **Saturn in Leo:** You express your authority nobly.

♅ **Uranus in Leo:** You express your inventiveness creatively.

♆ **Neptune in Leo:** You express your idealism dramatically.

♇ **Pluto in Leo:** You express your self-control dramatically.

♍
Virgo

☉ **Sun in Virgo:** Your ego expresses itself through service.

☽ **Moon in Virgo:** Your personality expresses itself through service.

☿ ***Mercury in Virgo:** You think analytically.

♀ **Venus in Virgo:** You love to be needed.

♂ **Mars in Virgo:** Your energies are channeled mentally.

♃ **Jupiter in Virgo:** You express your generosity through service.

♄ **Saturn in Virgo:** You are serious about your work.

♅ **Uranus in Virgo:** You express your inventiveness at work.

♆ **Neptune in Virgo:** You dream of being needed.

♇ **Pluto in Virgo:** Transformation occurs through service.

♎
Libra

☉ **Sun in Libra:** Your ego comes alive in partnership.

☽ **Moon in Libra:** You are instinctively drawn to partnership.

☿ **Mercury in Libra:** Your thinking is balanced.

♀ ***Venus in Libra:** You love partnership.

♂ **Mars in Libra:** You are aggressive in partnership.

♃ **Jupiter in Libra:** Your generosity is balanced.

♄ **Saturn in Libra:** You express your authority in partnership.

♅ **Uranus in Libra:** Your individuality can shake up your partnerships.

♆ **Neptune in Libra:** You dream of partnership.

♇ **Pluto in Libra:** Your attitude toward partnership undergoes a total change.

♏
Scorpio

☉ **Sun in Scorpio:** Your ego is controlled.

☽ **Moon in Scorpio:** Your personality undergoes a transformation.

☿ **Mercury in Scorpio:** Your ideas are secretive.

♀ **Venus in Scorpio:** Your love nature is controlled.

♂ ***Mars in Scorpio:** Your passions are very intense.

♃ **Jupiter in Scorpio:** You have many secrets.

♄ **Saturn in Scorpio:** Your fear will be transformed.

♅ **Uranus in Scorpio:** Your rebelliousness undergoes a change.

♆ **Neptune in Scorpio:** Your dreams are intense.

♇ **Pluto in Scorpio:** Your need to control will be transformed.

↗
Sagittarius

☉ **Sun in Sagittarius:** Your ego wants to be free.

☽ **Moon in Sagittarius:** You are instinctively drawn to distant places.

☿ **Mercury in Sagittarius:** Your thinking is philosophical.

♀ **Venus in Sagittarius:** Your love is free and unbound.

♂ **Mars in Sagittarius:** Your energies are directed philosophically.

♃ ***Jupiter in Sagittarius:** Your friendship is expansive.

♄ **Saturn in Sagittarius:** You want your authority to expand.

♅ **Uranus in Sagittarius:** You rebel on principle.

♆ **Neptune in Sagittarius:** You dream of being free.

♇ **Pluto in Sagittarius:**   Your principles undergo a total change.

♑
Capricorn

☉ **Sun in Capricorn:**   Your ego is conservative.

☽ **Moon in Capricorn:**   Your moods are serious.

☿ **Mercury in Capricorn:**   Your ideas are traditional.

♀ **Venus in Capricorn:**   Your love nature is conservative.

♂ **Mars in Capricorn:**   Your passion is restricted.

♃ **Jupiter in Capricorn:**   Your generosity is limited.

♄ ***Saturn in Capricorn:**   Your attitude toward responsibility is traditional.

♅ **Uranus in Capricorn:**   Your inventiveness is restricted.

♆ **Neptune in Capricorn:**   Your dreams are limited.

♇ **Pluto in Capricorn:**   You transform authority and tradition.

♒
Aquarius

☉ **Sun in Aquarius:** Your ego is a combination of the traditional and the unique.

☽ **Moon in Aquarius:** Your moods are unpredictable

☿ **Mercury in Aquarius:** Your ideas are inventive.

♀ **Venus in Aquarius:** You love humanity.

♂ **Mars in Aquarius:** You express your energy both traditionally and originally.

♃ **Jupiter in Aquarius:** You are generous with humanity.

♄ **Saturn in Aquarius:** Your attitude toward authority is original.

♅ ***Uranus in Aquarius:** Your inventiveness in unpredictable.

♆ **Neptune in Aquarius:** Your originality expresses itself behind the scenes.

♇ **Pluto in Aquarius:** Your inventiveness is completely transformed.

♓
Pisces

☉ **Sun in Pisces:** Your ego expresses itself idealistically.

☽ **Moon in Pisces:** Your moods are inspired.

☿ **Mercury in Pisces:** Your thoughts are idealistic.

♀ **Venus in Pisces:** Your love is spiritual.

♂ **Mars in Pisces:** Your energies dissipate.

♃ ***Jupiter in Pisces:** Your generosity is idealistic.

♄ **Saturn in Pisces:** You are serious about spirituality.

♅ **Uranus in Pisces:** You are rebellious about spiritual matters.

♆ **Neptune in Pisces:** You are deeply spiritual.

♇ **Pluto in Pisces:** You transform spiritually.

Now That I've Cast It, **What** Do I Do With It?

ASPECTS
BETWEEN PLANETS

ASPECTS ARE THE RELATIONSHIPS between planets and indicate whether the principles they represent will function with ease or difficulty. While the traditionally malefic aspects (square, opposition, quincunx) are supposed to be difficult, and the traditionally benefic aspects (trine, sextile) are supposed to be easy, there are those who accept the challenges presented by the so-called difficult aspects and use them to their benefit.

The Aspects

△ **Trine (120°):**   an aspect of luck.

✶ **Sextile (60°):**   an aspect of opportunity.

☌ **Conjunction (Two**   this is the strongest aspect
planets next to one   of all. The planets involved
another within 10°):   in the conjunction as well
as the planets that aspect
it determine the ease or
difficulty with which the
lessons will be learned.

☍ **Opposition (180°):**   an aspect of balance or
separation.

□ **Square (90°):**   this aspect presents a
challenge to be faced.

⚻ **Quincunx or**   an aspect of adjustment or
Inconjunct (150°):   separation.

A simple illustration of the aspects will help you understand them. Let's pretend that I have a box of cookies which I give to you as a gift. You do not have to earn the cookies or give me anything in return. All you have to do is sit there and receive them. That is the trine, or luck, aspect.

Let's now imagine that I enter the room with the same box of cookies. I am willing to give them to you if you will simply get up out of your seat and come get them. You have an opportunity to receive a gift, but must exert a small amount of effort in the process. This is the sextile, or opportunity, aspect.

Let's change the scene and imagine that you have a cake that I want. I am willing to exchange my cookies for it, but if you won't give me the cake, I won't give you the cookies. We must work in cooperation with each other in order to get what we want. This is the opposition, or balancing, aspect.

Let's modify the previous scene and imagine that I enter the room empty-handed, run over to you, and grab your cake. You now have a decision to make. You can either run after me and try to get your cake back, possibly risking a fight in the process, or you can do nothing and just be angry. A different alternative might be to make the most of the situation and realize that this is a golden opportunity to begin that diet you've been meaning to start. In this way, you can benefit from what at first appeared to be a problem. This is the challenge of the square. Your reaction to it determines whether it remains a problem or an opportunity for growth.

If I enter the room and plop myself onto your lap, you and I form a conjunction. This aspect is variable and depends on the planets involved. If you are a happy person who enjoys a good laugh, our being conjunct will not bother you at all, but if you are a serious person and do not like the idea that I am sitting on your lap, our being conjunct will annoy you. Conjunctions are also affected by the aspects they make to the rest of the chart. Let's say that you are a neutral type of person, neither serious nor happy. When I drop myself onto your lap, it neither makes you laugh nor upsets you, but a negative reaction from someone else triggers a negative reaction in you. This illustrates a square acting on a conjunction. A trine or sextile to a conjunction would be someone triggering a positive reaction in you.

The quincunx (often called the inconjunct) involves an element of adjustment. If this adjustment is not made, a separation can result. For example, if I knew that you were on a diet and, nevertheless, offered you some cookies, you could refuse and I would be left with the cookies. However, if I "adjusted" my offer and, instead of cookies, offered you whatever your diet permitted, you would accept my gift.

The best way to understand aspects is to understand the principles the planets teach within the framework of the aspect. Harmonious aspects help the principle manifest positively, while inharmonious aspects cause them to function negatively.

The following lists describe the principles taught by each of the planets. Combine any word from one planetary category with any word from its opposite category, link them up in a BASIC SENTENCE, and you will better understand the interactions between the two planets.

☉
The Sun

Positive Expression	Negative Expression
Creativity	Self-will
Individuality	Egocentricity
Strength	Dictatorialness
Dignity	Overbearingness
Vitality	Overconfidence
Leadership	Abuse of power
Pride	Self-centeredness

☽
The Moon

Positive Expression	Negative Expression
Protectiveness	Moodiness
Intuition	Changeability
Positive Emotions	Negative Emotions
Personality	Emotional Insecurity
Imagination	Emotional Over-reaction

Sensitivity	Over-protectiveness
Subconscious Mind	Negative Instincts
Instincts	Emotional Reactions

☿
Mercury

Positive Expression	**Negative Expression**
Ideas, Thoughts	Talkativeness
Words	Nervousness
Verbal Ability	Restlessness
Mental Ability	Criticalness
Conscious Mind	Indecisiveness

♀
Venus

Positive Expression	**Negative Expression**
Beauty	Self-indulgence
Love	Laziness
Art	Phoniness
Charm	Ostentation
Pleasure	Superficiality
Affection	
Courtesy	
Sweetness	

♂
Mars

Positive Expression	**Negative Expression**
Energy	Hate
Action	Impatience

Passion	Negative Sexuality
Spontaneity	Anger
Fearlessness	Cruelty
Frankness	Selfishness
Impulsiveness	Recklessness

♃
Jupiter

Positive Expression / **Negative Expression**

Positive Expression	Negative Expression
Optimism	Over-optimism
Friendship	Overbearingness
Friendliness	Exaggeration
Abundance	Rationalizing
Justice	Extravagance
Generosity	Over-abundance
Expansiveness	Over-indulgence
Enthusiasm	

♄
Saturn

Positive Expression	Negative Expression
Responsibility	Restriction
Discipline	Limitation
Maturity	Cruelty
Thriftiness	Dominance
Respect	Depression
Authority	Stinginess
Crystallization	Rigidity
Strength	Fear
Tradition	

⛢
Uranus

Positive Expression

Inventiveness

Non-conformity

Individuality

Unpredictability

Psychic ability

Negative Expression

Rebelliousness

Eccentricity

Irresponsibility

Unpredictability

Explosiveness

Negative Psychism

♆
Neptune

Positive Expression

Idealism

Spirituality

Dreams

Inspiration

Service

Sacrifice

Negative Expression

Daydreaming

Martyrdom

Escapism

Self-indulgence

Self-deception

Wishful Thinking

♇
Pluto

Positive Expression

Metamorphosis

Transmutation

Transformation

Self-control

Intensity

Psychism

Negative Expression

Upheaval

Destruction

Manipulation

Control

Rebellion

Psychic Abuse

Vengeance

Here are some suggested BASIC SENTENCES for the planetary aspects.

☉
THE SUN
Positive Aspects, Including Conjunctions

☽ **Moon:**   Your emotions are creative.

☿ **Mercury:** Your thinking is creative.

♀ **Venus:**   You are creative in love.

♂ **Mars:**   Your energies are used creatively.

♃ **Jupiter:** You create happiness around you.

♄ **Saturn:**   You use your authority creatively.

♅ **Uranus:**   You are proud of your individuality.

♆ **Neptune:** You are proud of your idealism.

♇ **Pluto:**   You are proud of your self-control.

Negative Aspects, Including Conjunctions

☽ **Moon:**   Your moods can be self-destructive.

☿ **Mercury:** Your thinking can be self-centered.

♀ **Venus:**   You can indulge yourself.

♂ **Mars:**   Your anger can be overbearing.

♃ **Jupiter:** Your self-will can be excessive.

♄ **Saturn:**   Your ego can be rigid.

♅ **Uranus:**   Your rebelliousness can be egocentric.

♆ **Neptune:** You can be proud of your martyrdom.

♇ **Pluto:**   You can be proud of your ability to manipulate.

(NOTE: While the Sun and Mercury, and the Sun and Venus can never afflict one another, afflictions between these planets can occur as a result of mutual receptions.)

☽
THE MOON
Positive Aspects, Including Conjunctions

☿ **Mercury:** Your mind is intuitive.

♀ **Venus:**   You are instinctively loving.

♂ **Mars:**   Your emotions respond quickly.

♃ **Jupiter:** You are protective in friendship.

♄ **Saturn:**   You are protective of traditions.

♅ **Uranus:**   You are intuitively inventive.

♆ **Neptune:** You are inspired intuitively.

♇ **Pluto:**   You can control your moods.

Negative Aspects, Including Conjunctions

☿ **Mercury:** You can change your mind easily.

♀ **Venus:**   You can be over-protective in love.

♂ **Mars:**   You can be impatient and moody.

♃ **Jupiter:** You can rationalize to protect yourself.

♄ **Saturn:**   You can be moody and easily depressed.

♅ **Uranus:**   Your emotions can make you rebellious.

♆ **Neptune:** You can indulge in emotional escapism.

♇ **Pluto:**   You can manipulate others emotionally.

☿

MERCURY
Positive Aspects, Including Conjunctions

♀ **Venus:**   Your thinking is artistic.

♂ **Mars:**   You have a quick mind.

♃ **Jupiter:**   You have many ideas.

♄ **Saturn:**   Your thinking is disciplined.

♅ **Uranus:**   Your thinking is inventive.

♆ **Neptune:** Your thinking is inspired.

♇ **Pluto:**   Your thinking is psychic.

Negative Aspects, Including Conjunctions

♀ **Venus:**   Your thinking can be self-indulgent.

♂ **Mars:**   You can speak very sharply.

♃ **Jupiter:**   You can talk excessively.

♄ **Saturn:**   Your thinking can be rigid.

♅ **Uranus:**   Your ideas can be rebellious.

♆ **Neptune:** Your thinking can be self-deceptive.

♇ **Pluto:**   Your ideas can be destructive.

(NOTE: While Mercury and Venus can never afflict one another, afflictions between them can occur as a result of mutual receptions.)

♀
VENUS
Positive Aspects, Including Conjunctions

♂ **Mars:** Your love nature is spontaneous.

♃ **Jupiter:** You are loving and generous.

♄ **Saturn:** You are loyal when it comes to love.

♅ **Uranus:** You have an original sense of beauty.

♆ **Neptune:** Your love is spiritual.

♇ **Pluto:** You love very deeply.

Negative Aspects, Including Conjunctions

♂ **Mars:** You can be selfish in love.

♃ **Jupiter:** You can rationalize your self-indulgence.

♄ **Saturn:** You can be fearful of love.

♅ **Uranus:** You can be irresponsible in love.

♆ **Neptune:** You can be (self-) deceptive in love.

♇ **Pluto:** You can be resentful and manipulative in love.

♂
MARS
Positive Aspects, Including Conjunctions

♃ **Jupiter:** You are spontaneously generous.

♄ **Saturn:** You are frank and authoritative.

♅ **Uranus:** You are actively inventive.

♆ **Neptune:**   You receive spontaneous inspiration.

♇ **Pluto:**   Your passions are under control.

Negative Aspects, Including Conjunctions

♃ **Jupiter:**   You can be recklessly extravagant.

♄ **Saturn:**   You can be angry and cruel.

♅ **Uranus:**   Your temper can be explosive.

♆ **Neptune:**   You can selfishly escape.

♇ **Pluto:**   Your anger and vengeance can be powerful.

♃
JUPITER
Positive Aspects, Including Conjunctions

♄ **Saturn:**   You are generous and mature.

♅ **Uranus:**   You are very much an individual.

♆ **Neptune:**   You have a great deal of inspiration.

♇ **Pluto:**   Your expansiveness is under control.

Negative Aspects, Including Conjunctions

♄ **Saturn:**   Your generosity fights with your stinginess.

♅ **Uranus:**   You are overly rebellious.

♆ **Neptune:**   You can exaggerate your own spirituality.

♇ **Pluto:**   Your generosity fights with your control.

♄
SATURN
Positive Aspects, Including Conjunctions

♅ **Uranus:** Your individuality expresses itself conservatively.

♆ **Neptune:** Your inspiration is practical.

♇ **Pluto:** You are controlled and disciplined.

Negative Aspects, Including Conjunctions

♅ **Uranus:** You can be both rigid and rebellious, which produces frustration.

♆ **Neptune:** You can experience both depression and fear.

♇ **Pluto:** You can resent authority figures.

♅
URANUS
Positive Aspects, Including Conjunctions

♆ **Neptune:** You are inventive and intuitive.

♇ **Pluto:** Your psychic ability is strong.

Negative Aspects, Including Conjunctions

♆ **Neptune:** You can be unpredictable and self-deceptive.

♇ **Pluto:** You can become suddenly rebellious.

ASPECTS TO ANGLES

TO UNDERSTAND HOW TO INTERPRET the angles when planets make aspect to them, simply apply the same rules we just used when we took aspect from planet to planet. Keep in mind that while a planet in the 7th house and close to that cusp will operate in the 7th house, it is also in opposition to the ascendant. The same holds true for a planet in the 4th house and close to the cusp. It is in opposition to the *mc* (the cusp of the 10th house). The ascendant is the most personal point in the chart. It is the YOU of the chart, and describes your body, your physical appearance and your personality. I have seen charts in which the ascendant was more powerful than the Sun because of the Sun's placement. The *mc* describes your public image, your career and the way the world sees you.

TO ASCENDANT
Positive Aspects, Including Conjunctions

☉ **Sun**   You have personal strength.

☽ **Moon**   You have good intuition.

☿ **Mercury** You have good ideas.

♀ **Venus**   You can be charming and beautiful/handsome.

♂ **Mars**   You have lots of energy.

♃ **Jupiter**   You are generous and optimistic.

♄ **Saturn**   You are mature and responsible.

♅ **Uranus**   You are inventive.

♆ **Neptune** You are inspired.

♇ **Pluto**   You are self-controlled.

Negative Aspects, Including Conjunctions

☉ **Sun**   You can be self-centered.

☽ **Moon**   You can be overly self-protective.

☿ **Mercury** You can be overly talkative.

♀ **Venus**   You can be self-indulgent.

♂ **Mars**   You can be impatient and angry.

♃ **Jupiter**   You can be overbearing.

♄ **Saturn**   You can be depressing.

♅ **Uranus**   You can be unpredictable and rebellious.

♆ **Neptune** You can daydream.

♇ **Pluto**   You can be manipulative.

TO MC
Positive Aspects, Including Conjunctions

☉ **Sun**   Your ability to lead can help your career.

☽ **Moon**   Your intuition can help your career.

☿ **Mercury** Your ideas can help your career.

♀ **Venus**   Your chart can help your career.

♂ **Mars**   Your energy can help your career.

♃ **Jupiter**   Your optimism can help your career.

♄ **Saturn**   Your maturity can help your career.

♅ **Uranus**   Your inventiveness can help your career.

♆ **Neptune** Your inspiration can help your career.

♇ **Pluto**   Your self-control can help your career.

Negative Aspects, Including Conjunctions

☉ **Sun**   Self-centeredness can hinder your career.

☽ **Moon**   Moodiness can hinder your career.

☿ **Mercury** Talkativeness can hinder your career.

♀ **Venus**   Overindulgence can hinder your career.

♂ **Mars**   Temper can hinder your career.

♃ **Jupiter**   Exaggeration can hinder your career.

♄ **Saturn**   Rigidity can hinder your career.

♅ **Uranus**   Unpredictability can hinder your career.

♆ **Neptune**   Daydreaming can hinder your career.

♇ **Pluto**   The need for control can hinder your career.

LINKING PLANETS
WITH SIGNS

A N ADDED DIMENSION TO CHART interpretation is the linking of the planets with the signs they rule. Keep in mind that the signs are the principles to be learned. The house cusp on which a sign falls tells us the area of life in which that principle will be learned. Often, that principle will express itself in more than one area of lie. That is where the planet comes in, for as the ruler or roving delegate of that sign, it acts as a messenger, carrying the sign's message to the house in question.

For example, if Cancer is on the 11th cusp and the Moon is in the 2nd house, the energy begins in the 11th and expresses itself in the 2nd. Keeping in mind that the ruler of the 11th is in the 2nd, we compose a BASIC SENTENCE which will link the two. Our thinking might go like this: the 11th house ruler is in the 2nd. The 11th house sends its energy to the 2nd. The 11th house rules friends, hopes, wishes and groups. The 2nd house rules values, possessions, money and talents. Therefore, we could say that our friends influence our values. (Notice that I did not say that our values influence our friends. This is because the energy is traveling from the 11th to the 2nd, and not from the 2nd to the 11th. Notice, too, that I did not use Aquarius as the ruler of the 11th house because we are not talking about the natural ruler, but about the sign that happens to be on the 11th cusp.) Some BASIC SENTENCES that apply to this example are: Our friends can help us earn money. Our friends influence our values. Our friends are our possessions. Our friends trigger our talents. Our friends make us acquisitive.

Keep in mind that it makes no difference what sign falls on the cusp in question. We simply link the sign with its ruler's house position. For example, we could use the very same BASIC SENTENCES we just composed if Gemini were on the 11th cusp and Mercury were in the 2nd house. The ruler of the 11th still falls in the 2nd.

The following suggested BASIC SENTENCES should help you link the planets with their signs. As with all BASIC SENTENCES, they are suggestions, and some of them may need modification in order to apply.

RULER OF THE FIRST

Ruler of the 1st in the 1st: You identify with YOU. You have a strong self-interest.

Ruler of the 1st in the 2nd: You identify with money. You are your own possession. It's hard to let go of yourself.

Ruler of the 1st in the 3rd: You identify with your ideas. You think and talk about yourself.

Ruler of the 1st in the 4th: You identify with your home and family.

Ruler of the 1st in the 5th: You identify with children.

Ruler of the 1st in the 6th: You identify with your work.

Ruler of the 1st in the 7th: You identify with your spouse. You influence others.

Ruler of the 1st in the 8th: You identify with the unknown, with the psychic. You will experience a personal transformation.

Ruler of the 1st in the 9th: You identify with God and your principles.

Ruler of the 1st in the 10th: You identify with authority figures, with your career.

Ruler of the 1st in the 11th: You identify with friends and groups.

Ruler of the 1st in the 12th: You identify with behind-the-scenes activities and service.

RULER OF THE SECOND

Ruler of the 2nd in the 1st: Your values influence your personality. You spend money on yourself.

Ruler of the 2nd in the 2nd: Your values and possessions are very important to you.

Ruler of the 2nd in the 3rd: You talk about your possessions and values. You have money on your mind.

Ruler of the 2nd in the 4th: You spend money on your home and family. You spend money on what makes you feel secure.

Ruler of the 2nd in the 5th: You spend money on your children and pleasurable activities.

Ruler of the 2nd in the 6th: You put your money into your work. Your values are reflected in your work.

Ruler of the 2nd in the 7th: You influence others with your values. You spend money on your spouse.

Ruler of the 2nd in the 8th: Your values influence your partner's values. Your values will be transformed.

Ruler of the 2nd in the 9th: You can spend money on higher education, travel, or in pursuit of your philosophy of life.

Ruler of the 2nd in the 10th: You put your money and energies into your career. Your values come to the attention of the public.

Ruler of the 2nd in the 11th: You give your possessions to your friends. You spend money on your friends.

Ruler of the 2nd in the 12th: You take your money and hide it, i.e., you have hidden resources.

RULER OF THE THIRD

Ruler of the 3rd in the 1st: Your ideas are centered around yourself. You think and talk about yourself.

Ruler of the 3rd in the 2nd: Your mind turns to money-making ideas. You talk about money. You can make money through your ideas.

Ruler of the 3rd in the 3rd: You have many ideas and must express them.

Ruler of the 3rd in the 4th: You think of your home and family. You share your ideas with your family.

Ruler of the 3rd in the 5th: You think of fun and games. You have creative ideas. You share your ideas with your children.

Ruler of the 3rd in the 6th: You think of your work and health. You share your ideas with your employees.

Ruler of the 3rd in the 7th: You influence others with your ideas. You think of marriage and partnership.

Ruler of the 3rd in the 8th: Your thinking will undergo a transformation. You think deeply. Your ideas can influence other people's values.

Ruler of the 3rd in the 9th: You think of travel and expansion. You think philosophically. You see the big picture.

Ruler of the 3rd in the 10th: You think of your career. You express your ideas to those in authority.

Ruler of the 3rd in the 11th: You think of your friends. You share your ideas with your friends.

Ruler of the 3rd in the 12th: Your thoughts are hidden. Your conscious mind is in tune with your subconscious mind.

RULER OF THE FOURTH

Ruler of the 4th in the 1st: Your family influences you strongly. Your need for security affects you personally.

Ruler of the 4th in the 2nd: Your home and family are your possessions. You can earn money through real estate. Your family influences your values.

Ruler of the 4th in the 3rd: Your family, especially the 4th house parent, influences your thinking.

Ruler of the 4th in the 4th: Your home, family and security are very important to you.

Ruler of the 4th in the 5th: Your 4th house parent can be like a child to you or may influence your children.

Ruler of the 4ᵗʰ in the 6ᵗʰ: Your need for security can be fulfilled through work/service. Your 4ᵗʰ house parent can influence the type of work you do and may be involved in your work.

Ruler of the 4ᵗʰ in the 7ᵗʰ: Your security need is fulfilled in partnership. You project your 4ᵗʰ house parent onto your spouse.

Ruler of the 4ᵗʰ in the 8ᵗʰ: Your security need will undergo a transformation, as will your attitude toward home and family.

Ruler of the 4ᵗʰ in the 9ᵗʰ: Your need for security can be fulfilled through travel, study and/or living according to your principles. Your home can be far from your place of birth.

Ruler of the 4ᵗʰ in the 10ᵗʰ: Your 4ᵗʰ house parent becomes the 10ᵗʰ house parent, assuming both roles. Your security need is fulfilled by being an authority figure/having a career.

Ruler of the 4ᵗʰ in the 11ᵗʰ: Your need for security can be fulfilled through friends and group activities. Your 4ᵗʰ house parent can be like a friend and/or influence your choice of friends.

Ruler of the 4ᵗʰ in the 12ᵗʰ: Your need for security is hidden, perhaps, even from yourself. It can be worked out through behind-the-scenes service.

RULER OF THE FIFTH

Ruler of the 5ᵗʰ in the 1ˢᵗ: Your children have a direct influence on you. Your creative urges and dramatic ability are reflected n your personality.

Ruler of the 5th in the 2nd: Your children influence your values. Your children are your possessions. You can make money through creative projects and/or speculation.

Ruler of the 5th in the 3rd: Your creativity influences your thinking. Romance colors your thoughts. Your children influence your ideas.

Ruler of the 5th in the 4th: Your children may act more like your parents as time goes by. You can entertain and express your creative talents in your home.

Ruler of the 5th in the 5th: You have strong romantic and creative urges. You love to have fun.

Ruler of the 5th in the 6th: You can express your creativity in your work. You can deal with children at work.

Ruler of the 5th in the 7th: Your child is your equal. Your child is like a partner to you.

Ruler of the 5th in the 8th: Your attitude toward children will be transformed. Your desire for fun will change.

Ruler of the 5th in the 9th: Your social life can involve long-distance relationships. Your children influence your principles.

Ruler of the 5th in the 10th: You can express your creativity in your career. Your career can deal with children.

Ruler of the 5th in the 11th: Your children are like friends to you. You can express your creativity in groups.

Ruler of the 5ᵗʰ in the 12ᵗʰ: There is a hidden element to your love life. Your concept of romance is private and personal.

RULER OF THE SIXTH

Ruler of the 6ᵗʰ in the 1ˢᵗ: Your work is part of you. Your work directly affects your health.

Ruler of the 6ᵗʰ in the 2ⁿᵈ: Your work makes money for you and influences your values. Your work is your possession.

Ruler of the 6ᵗʰ in the 3ʳᵈ: Your employees influence your thinking. Your work is always on your mind.

Ruler of the 6ᵗʰ in the 4ᵗʰ: You take your work home with you. You can work out of your home. Your work fulfills your security needs.

Ruler of the 6ᵗʰ in the 5ᵗʰ: Your work may involve children. Your health influences your creative ability. Your work has to be fun.

Ruler of the 6ᵗʰ in the 6ᵗʰ: Work, health and providing a necessary service are all very important to you.

Ruler of the 6ᵗʰ in the 7ᵗʰ: Your work can involve dealing with the public. You may provide a one-on-one service in your work.

Ruler of the 6ᵗʰ in the 8ᵗʰ: Your work can involve the psychic. Your work can undergo a total change. Your work can involve helping others with their finances or resources.

Ruler of the 6th in the 9th: Your work can involve long-distance travel or higher education. You must work at something you believe in.

Ruler of the 6th in the 10th: Your work comes to the attention of the public. You want to serve from a position of authority and importance.

Ruler of the 6th in the 11th: You want to serve and be needed by your friends. You can work for a group.

Ruler of the 6th in the 12th: Your work takes place behind the scenes. You escape through your work. You serve through your work.

RULER OF THE SEVENTH

Ruler of the 7th in the 1st: Your partner influences you. Other people influence you.

Ruler of the 7th in the 2nd: Your partner influences your values. Your spouse is your possession. Partnership can be financially profitable for you.

Ruler of the 7th in the 3rd: Partnership is on your mind. Your spouse influences your thinking.

Ruler of the 7th in the 4th: Your partner is like a parent to you. Marriage fulfills your need for emotional security. You are "married" to your family.

Ruler of the 7th in the 5th: Your partner is like a child to you.

Your spouse inspires you to create. You are "married" to your children.

Ruler of the 7th in the 6th: Your partner influences your work. You may feel "married" to your job. Your work can involve the public.

Ruler of the 7th in the 7th: Partnership is very important to you.

Ruler of the 7th in the 8th: Your attitude toward marriage can undergo a total change.

Ruler of the 7th in the 9th: You are "married" to your philosophy. Your spouse influences your principles. To you, marriage involves a contract with God.

Ruler of the 7th in the 10th: You are "married" to your career. Your spouse is like your 10th house parent.

Ruler of the 7th in the 11th: You are "married" to your friends. Your spouse is your friend.

Ruler of the 7th in the 12th: There is a private element to your partnerships. Your partner influences you subconsciously.

RULER OF THE EIGHTH

Ruler of the 8th in the 1st: Other people's values influence you. Money can come to you through an inheritance.

Ruler of the 8th in the 2nd: Other people's finances can contribute to your own. Your spouse's values influence yours.

Ruler of the 8ᵗʰ in the 3ʳᵈ: There is a direct link between your psychic mind and your conscious mind. Other people's values influence your thinking.

Ruler of the 8ᵗʰ in the 4ᵗʰ: Your partner's money can fulfill your need for security. You can come into an inheritance later on in life.

Ruler of the 8ᵗʰ in the 5ᵗʰ: You are psychically inspired to create. Your romantic/sexual energy is strong. There can be an inheritance for your children.

Ruler of the 8ᵗʰ in the 6ᵗʰ: Sleep is very important in maintaining your health. Your work can involve other people's money.

Ruler of the 8ᵗʰ in the 7ᵗʰ: You can help others get in touch with their values. Your spouse identifies with his money/possessions.

Ruler of the 8ᵗʰ in the 8ᵗʰ: There is great power and intensity to your desire nature. You may have a strong need to be in control. You can be interested in psychic investigation.

Ruler of the 8ᵗʰ in the 9ᵗʰ: Dreams and mysticism are part of your philosophy. Your dreams may involve travel over great distances. Your beliefs may involve being in control.

Ruler of the 8ᵗʰ in the 10ᵗʰ: Your desire for control can be put to use in your career. You are driven to be in a position of power. Your psychic ability can be useful in your career.

Ruler of the 8ᵗʰ in the 11ᵗʰ: You are powerful in groups. You want to be in control in groups. You can help your friends transform their lives.

Ruler of the 8th in the 12th: You can control from behind the scenes. Other people's values influence you, perhaps without your being aware of it. You have a great need for privacy.

RULER OF THE NINTH

Ruler of the 9th in the 1st: Your principles influence your personality. You feel a direct connection with God.

Ruler of the 9th in the 2nd: Travel can bring money and influence your values. Higher education can increase your earning power. Your philosophy influences your values.

Ruler of the 9th in the 3rd: Your higher mind speaks directly to your conscious mind. Your principles influence your thinking. You express your beliefs.

Ruler of the 9th in the 4th: Your need for security is fulfilled by living according to your principles.

Ruler of the 9th in the 5th: You express your beliefs to your children. Travel can broaden your social life.

Ruler of the 9th in the 6th: You put your principles into action in your work. You must work at something you believe in.

Ruler of the 9th in the 7th: You influence others with your principles. Your beliefs involve treating others as equals.

Ruler of the 9th in the 8th: Your philosophy undergoes a total change. You believe in secrets, metaphysics, transformation and dreams.

Ruler of the 9th in the 9th: You have a strong identification with God. You must live according to your principles. You love to travel. You have an understanding of human nature.

Ruler of the 9th in the 10th: You want to put your principles to work in your career and bring them to the attention of the public. Your career can involve travel.

Ruler of the 9th in the 11th: Your philosophy involves being a friend. You can travel great distances to be with your friends.

Ruler of the 9th in the 12th: You keep your principles to yourself. You believe in behind-the-scenes service.

RULER OF THE TENTH

Ruler of the 10th in the 1st: You feel the influence of authority figures on you. You are influenced by powerful people.

Ruler of the 10th in the 2nd: Your career brings you money. Authority figures directly influence your values. Your career is your possession.

Ruler of the 10th in the 3rd: Your thinking is affected by the authority figures in your life. The 10th house parent can be more like a sibling to you.

Ruler of the 10th in the 4th: You feel the influence of authority figures in your home. The 10th house parent becomes like the 4th house parent. You career can involve real estate.

Ruler of the 10th in the 5th: Your creativity is influenced by the authority figures in your life. Your career can deal with children or creativity. You want to be important to your children.

Ruler of the 10th in the 6th: You want to be an authority figure in your work. Your career involves service.

Ruler of the 10th in the 7th: Your career can involve partnership, counseling or dealing with the public. You treat authority figures as equals.

Ruler of the 10th in the 8th: Your attitude toward authority figures and power undergoes a total change. Your career can involve research, investigation or the psychic.

Ruler of the 10th in the 9th: Your career involves living according to your principles. Your career can involve teaching, long distance travel and/or serving God in some way.

Ruler of the 10th in the 10th: You have a strong sense of authority and power. You are a natural leader. You have a strong respect for tradition.

Ruler of the 10th in the 11th: You want to be the leader with your friends. You can deal with groups in your career. Your goals involve power and authority.

Ruler of the 10th in the 12th: Your career can involve behind-the-scenes work and service to others. The influence of the authority figures in your life may not be apparent.

RULER OF THE ELEVENTH

Ruler of the 11th in the 1st: Your friends influence you strongly. You are a direct expression of your hopes and wishes.

Ruler of the 11th in the 2nd: You can earn money through your friends or groups. Your friends influence your values. You see your friends as belonging to you.

Ruler of the 11th in the 3rd: Your goals are on your mind. Your friends influence your thinking.

Ruler of the 11th in the 4th: A friend may be like a mother to you. Your friends are like family to you.

Ruler of the 11th in the 5th: You treat your friends like children. Your friends play an active part in your social life.

Ruler of the 11th in the 6th: Your work can involve being a friend or working with groups. Your friends can help you in your work. Your goals involve service.

Ruler of the 11th in the 7th: You treat your friends as your equals. A friend can become a partner. Your hopes and wishes involve marriage.

Ruler of the 11th in the 8th: Your goals, hopes and wishes can undergo a total change. Your friends may be involved in metaphysics.

Ruler of the 11th in the 9th: Your goals involve travel. Your philosophy involves being a friend.

Ruler of the 11ᵗʰ in the 10ᵗʰ: Group work can be part of your career. Your friends can influence your career. You want to be a friend in your career.

Ruler of the 11ᵗʰ in the 11ᵗʰ: Friendship and group activities play an important role in your life. Your goals involve being a friend.

Ruler of the 11ᵗʰ in the 12ᵗʰ: You keep your friendships private. Your goals may be hidden. You may not be aware of how much your friends influence you.

RULER OF THE TWELFTH

Ruler of the 12ᵗʰ in the 1ˢᵗ: Your personality is strongly influenced by your past. You express your subconscious desire to serve and be needed.

Ruler of the 12ᵗʰ in the 2ⁿᵈ: You can earn your money through service. Your past influences your values.

Ruler of the 12ᵗʰ in the 3ʳᵈ: Your subconscious speaks directly to your conscious mind, giving you a natural psychic ability. You think spiritually.

Ruler of the 12ᵗʰ in the 4ᵗʰ: Privacy can fulfill your security need. You serve your family.

Ruler of the 12ᵗʰ in the 5ᵗʰ: You are creatively inspired. You want to be of service to children.

Ruler of the 12ᵗʰ in the 6ᵗʰ: You want to serve in the work you do.

Ruler of the 12th in the 7th: You are willing to serve in partnership. You feel a strong connection from the past with your partners.

Ruler of the 12th in the 8th: You work out "unfinished business" from the past during sleep. Your past is made clear to you in dreams. You serve on the astral plane during sleep.

Ruler of the 12th in the 9th: Service is part of your belief system. You help people during your travels.

Ruler of the 12th in the 10th: You want to serve in your career. Your behind-the-scenes activities can come to the attention of the public.

Ruler of the 12th in the 11th: You want to serve your friends and the groups to which you belong.

Ruler of the 12th in the 12th: You have a strong need for solitude and a strong desire to serve. You can be very spiritual.

THE 13ᵀᴴ HOUSE
(TIDBITS)

DIGNITY, DETRIMENT, EXALTATION & FALL

I have found that it is wise not to count too literally on the promised blessing of having a planet in its sign of exaltation. If the planet is afflicted or weakened by house position, the exaltation can also be weakened. The converse holds true for a planet in its fall. A well-aspected, well-placed planet will function better than an afflicted planet.

AFFLICTIONS

So often we read that a particular planet is afflicted, and we wonder just how many squares, oppositions or quincunxes it takes for a planet to fall into this category. What I have found is that a planet is afflicted if we are unable to learn the lesson it is there to teach us. So it is actually up to us to decide whether or not one of our planets is afflicted. Often the person with many squares and oppositions in his chart is much stronger than the person with trines and sextiles because he has had to learn tough lessons. Having learned them, he has grown and can handle more than the person with an "easy" chart.

PATTERNS

While most people are familiar with what the ideal splash, bundle, locomotive, bowl, bucket and see-saw patterns look like, it is often difficult to categorize a particular chart because it deviates too much from the ideal. I have found that patterns to work—if you can identify the pattern!

MUTUAL RECEPTION

Two planets are in mutual reception when each is in the other's sign. To interpret a mutual reception, we first interpret the planets as they are in the chart. Then we mentally change places between them and place them in their own signs. Finally, we reinterpret them. For example, if someone has their Sun in 11 degrees of Virgo in the 9th house and Mercury in 15 degrees of Leo in the 10th house, the Sun and Mercury are in mutual reception because they are in each other's signs. We first interpret the chart as it is. Then we mentally change places between the two planets and interpret Mercury in 11 degrees of Virgo in the 10th and the Sun in 15 degrees of Leo in the 9th. You can see the added dimension this gives any chart.

THE CHARTS IN OUR CHARTS

We are able to see everyone in our lives in our own natal chart. We know that the 7th house is our mate, the 4th and 10th our parents, the 3rd our siblings, and the 5th our children, but these are not the only people we can see in the chart. We can literally see everyone who affects our lives and everything that affects theirs. For example, if the 1st house is you, then the 7th is your spouse. If the 2nd is your money, then the 8th is your spouse's money, etc.

What if you have been married more than once? You can see successive husbands (children, siblings, etc.) individually. Simply count two houses from the house in question. The house that you arrive at is the 1st house of the person or matter in questions. This means that your first spouse is your 7th house, your second spouse is your 9th house, your third spouse is your 11th house, etc.

The same rule holds true for our children. While the 5th house describes children in general, it also describes our first child in particular. Our second child is described by the 7th house, and our third child by the 9th house. This means that our second child will be teaching us the same lessons as our first husband. They can have many similarities and may be drawn to each other as well.

After finding the person in question, you can read their entire chart symbolically through your own. For example, if you are concerned about your mother's finances, but don't have her chart, look for her in your own. First decide whether she is represented by your 4th or 10th house. If she is your 4th house, your 5th house is her 2nd house of money.

Another example: you want to find out about your 3rd child's marriage potential. The 5th rules your children in general, and the first in particular. Since the 9th house rules your third child, her spouse is indicated by your 3rd house (the 7th from the 9th of the third child).

You can verify the accuracy of your findings by comparing them to the person's natal chart. If the charts are accurate, the information will dovetail.

RETROGRADE PLANETS

A retrograde planet in the natal chart manifests on a more introspective level than the other planets. When the retrograde planet goes direct by progression, it begins to function more expressively. When the progressed planet returns to its exact natal position, it seems to come alive. For example, let's say that Mercury is retrograde in your natal chart. This means that until Mercury went direct, you may have kept your thoughts to yourself. Perhaps you did not learn to walk or talk as quickly as other children. However, when you DID start to speak, you spoke full sentences, and when you started to walk, you were probably able to run without falling.

THE VERTEX AND ANTI-VERTEX

I first learned about the Vertex in 1970 from the late Charles A. Jayne who discovered it. He described it as our karmic role in life, and since it is always on the right-hand side of the chart, it is our karmic role with others. As he put it, if your role is to be a butler, you can be a happy butler, a sad butler, etc., but *you will be a butler.* Period. In other words, you cannot change your karmic role in life. The Vertex is the place in the chart where you have no control, i.e., it is fated. (This is not necessarily a negative thing.) It has been my observation that if the Vertex is the point over which you have no control, then the Anti-Vertex, which is directly opposite the Vertex and is always on the left side of the chart, is the point over which you DO have control. I use the Vertex and Anti-Vertex in chart comparisons and forecasts, and apply only conjunctions to them.

HELIOCENTRIC PLANETS

The natal chart is cast for the moment of birth—somewhere on planet earth. We view the planets from this vantage point. This is Geocentric astrology, and is what most astrologers use. However, since the Sun, not the earth, is the center of our galaxy, some people feel that we should use the Heliocentric placements of the planets. I use both. I insert Heliocentric Mercury, Venus and Mars into the traditional Geocentric chart. (The heavy planets are pretty much in the same place Heliocentrically as Geocentrically.) What convinced me to do this with all my clients was a chart I was working on in 1987. My client was an international businessman, and regularly flew back and forth to China. He had visited much of the world before he was 25, yet there was nothing in his chart to indicate this. So I looked at his Heliocentric planets—and Mars was in his 9th house! I was sold!

ABOUT MAXINE

MAXINE TAYLOR IS A TRUE PIONEER in the field of astrology. She began her astrological studies in 1966. In 1968, she became Georgia's first licensed astrologer. In 1969, she had a bill introduced into the Georgia General Assembly to legalize astrology in Atlanta. In 1970, the bill passed and was signed into law by the governor, making Atlanta the first city in the country to license the practice of astrology.

Maxine continued to make history by spearheading the establishment of the Atlanta Board of Astrology Examiners. In 1979, she discovered how to read the hidden parental messages we received as children in our birth charts. She learned how to release these messages and began sharing the technique with clients in private sessions and workshops. In 2003, she was ordained as a trans-denominational minister and expanded her career to include energy healing. Today, she practices Star Matrix, her own healing technique.

Maxine was CNN's on-air astrologer for several years and appeared as a guest on *The Larry King Show*. Maxine and her predictions have been broadcast on CNN, ABC, CBS and NBC, as well as national and international radio. She has been featured and profiled in publications across the country, including *The Wall Street Journal*.

Maxine is a published author, a national speaker, a radio host, and a co-founder of the Metropolitan Atlanta Astrological Society, the Atlanta Board of Astrology Examiners and the Atlanta Institute of Metaphysics. She served as President of the Metropolitan Atlanta Astrological Society, and Chairman of the Atlanta Board of Astrology Examiners. She is the author of several astrology reports for Cosmic Patterns and serves on the Board of Directors of the American Federation of Astrologers.

For a complete list of Maxine's services, you may contact her through her website: MaxineTaylor.com.

CPSIA information can be obtained
at www.ICGtesting.com
Printed in the USA
BVHW071611140120
569361BV00002B/131/P

9 780866 902038